CHAMBERS
Companion
to the
Burns Supper

Also available from Chambers

In the Land o' Burns
Poems and Songs of Robert Burns
Chambers Poetical Works of Robert Burns

CHAMBERS

Companion

to the

Burns Supper

Nancy Marshall

Chambers

Published 1992 by W & R Chambers Ltd,
43–45 Annandale Street, Edinburgh EH7 4AZ

British Library Cataloguing in Publication Data

A catalogue record for this book is
available from the British Library.

ISBN 0-550-21025-3

Acknowledgments

I should like to thank the following for their words
of advice: the Burns Federation; Andrew Winton,
Secretary, Edinburgh Burns Club; and especially
Mrs Martha McKellar, Secretary of the Ayr Burns Club.

Cover design and illustrations by John Marshall

Typeset by Alphaset Graphics Ltd, Edinburgh

Printed in Great Britain by Clays Ltd, St Ives plc

Contents

Preface

This book has been written for those who have never been to a Burns Supper and also would rather not attend their first one without possessing any knowledge of the form or substance of such an occasion. The elaborate ritual of Burns Night can be mystifying to the newcomer. The following will hopefully shed some light on this old Scots tradition and enable it to be enjoyed to the full.

Here the form of a traditional Burns Supper is spelled out in simple terms according to the best authorities on the subject: the Burns Federation and some of the oldest Burns clubs in existence. In addition you will find material to help you organize your own supper or even deliver an 'Immortal Memory' speech, should you be willing to try.

An evening to celebrate the life and works of Robert Burns is a worthwhile way to share good company. It should be both serious and fun. If this volume helps you to to it with confidence, it will have served its purpose.

The Life of Robert Burns
(1759-96)

Burns – the man and the poet

Robert Burns was born on 25 January 1759 in the Ayrshire village of Alloway. Most of the following 37 years, until his death in 1796, were spent working on the land, from farm labourer on his father's farms to farmer himself. Only during the last five years of his life, while acting as an exciseman in Dumfries, did he manage to free himself from the burden of toiling in the fields and even then, as he laid down the yoke of the soil for the last time, it was merely to travel the 200 miles a week on horseback needed to perform his excise duties. Life was never easy for Robert Burns. But whatever came his way, good or bad, pleasure or pain, he hungrily took it up like the artist he was, and celebrated the experience. His dogged determination in everything is reflected in the power of his work. Whether describing the instantaneous pleasure, the sad memory or the fleeting joy, he seems to capture and illuminate these feelings. His acute perception of life and everything and everyone around him originated in the early years he spent labouring on his father's farms. The fires of injustice were kindled in him as year after year of toil brought the family no relief from their daily hardship and the threat of the factor, and eviction for non-payment of rent always loomed in the background. The pain of these days, both physical and mental, was etched for ever into his mind. It was the source of his quick-silver mood changes, his depressions and melancholia. But more importantly it was the cradle of his creativity.

Robert Burns was a complex character, a loyal friend, a dangerous enemy with a fast, biting tongue, a caring and loving father, a hardworking farmer, a great debater who needed social stimulus as much as he craved the quiet and solitude of his own fireside; he was neither a fool regarding how others saw him, nor was he the uneducated 'ploughman poet' he allowed himself to be mistaken for.

Burns drank, but probably no more to excess than was the norm for the day. He had a way with the ladies, but as he describes in 'Address to the Unco Guid, or the Rigidly Righteous', the only reason some resist temptation is that temptation is never put in their way. The power of his work has stood the test of time, the sentiments in it as valid today as they have ever been. He combined intellect with imagination and instinct, and never lost his sense of justice, which gave him the freedom to expound his beliefs and loudly proclaim life's pleasures and passions.

In a country being overrun by English ways and customs and English government, the average Scotsman in Burns's time felt his way of life slipping away. Writing in the everyday language still used by the mass of the population, Burns avowed that their culture was still alive and in so doing elevated their existence and their pride in that existence. The gap he filled was a mixture of hope for the future and a nostalgia for the past, rather like the sentiments expressed in 'Auld Lang Syne'.

Family history

Robert Burns's father, William Burnes, settled in Ayrshire in 1750 but hailed originally from Kincardineshire, in the north-east of Scotland. His family had been tenant farmers on the estate of Earl Marischal, a staunch Stuart supporter. In later life, the romantic in Burns liked to believe that his ancestors' fall on hard times was due to their loyalty to the Jacobite cause, rather than such mundane reasons as his grandfather's over ambitious farming ventures or a succession of bad harvests. Whatever the reasons, the Burnes's household was broken up in 1748 due to bankruptcy, and the sons, William and Robert, went elsewhere in search of work. The poet's father, William, walked to Edinburgh and found work as a gardener, being employed for a time in helping to lay out 'the Meadows'. In 1750 he moved to Ayrshire on the west coast of Scotland, where he continued as a gardener: first for the Laird of Fairlee, then with the Crawfords of Doonside and finally at Doonholm for Dr Fergusson. During this time, this determined, hardworking man put aside enough money to lease seven and a half acres of land in Alloway, where he planned to build a house and set up as a market gardener. He continued working at Doonholm, while he began his market garden, and in 1757, just seven years after his arrival in Ayrshire, during the summer and autumn, he built, with his own hands, the 'auld clay biggin', known all over the world today as Burns Cottage. It was built as a home for his bride Agnes Brown, the daughter of an Ayrshire tenant farmer, whom he married on 15 December 1757. By then William Burnes was 36 years of age and his new wife 25. He was a slim, wiry figure of medium height and she was a small, vivacious redhead. They both possessed strong tempers, both had the ethos of hard work stamped through them and, probably because of their 'late' marriage, they both brought maturity and stability to a relationship which survived happily until William's death in 1784. Robert, the first of their seven children, was born on 25 January 1759.

Burns Cottage

Alloway

In Alloway the family's life passed pleasantly. While William Burnes continued to work as a gardener and run his small market garden, his wife looked after the dairy, and along with her cousin, Betty Davidson, entertained the children with old Scottish songs and tall tales, which, unknown to them, were to stimulate Burns's imagination and influence his work all his days. In 1765, at the age of six, and with his younger brother Gilbert, Robert entered the village school of Alloway for his first formal education. Sadly, after little more than a month, the schoolmaster left for Ayr and the school closed. An ever-resourceful William Burnes quickly got together with the heads of four other families and found a new master for the school, arranging that they split the cost of his salary between them and take it in turns to board him.

Mount Oliphant

John Murdoch, the young man who filled the post, regarded Robert and Gilbert as bright and hardworking. Gilbert of the two he thought had a 'more lively imagination' and was 'more of the wit, than Robert', and musically he found 'Robert's ear, in particular, was remarkably dull, and his voice untunable'. Murdoch continued to teach the boys for a time, although only sporadically, after the family moved to Mount Oliphant Farm early in 1766. By then William Burnes thought the cottage too small for his growing family and, to prevent his children becoming labourers and therefore 'underlings' in another household, he leased Mount Oliphant, a few miles from Alloway, at 40 pounds per year, becoming a tenant farmer like his ancestors. And he was to fare no better. In these 70 acres of exhausted soil, which hardly covered the rocks beneath, the family toiled in backbreaking work and lived in extreme frugality for the next 12 years. During that time, Robert performed a man's work, when he was still little more than a child, and in the process irreversibly damaged his heart. He described his time there as being 'the cheerless gloom of a hermit, with the unceasing moil of a galley slave'. Gilbert believed that Robert's later melancholia and the depressions which haunted him all his adult life stemmed from this time. Describing Robert's physical condition he said, 'At this time he was almost constantly afflicted in the evenings with a dull headache, which, at a subsequent period of his life, was exchanged for a palpitation of the heart, and a threatening of fainting and suffocation in the night time.' Robert's drastic measures to stop the palpitations included keeping a bucket of water at his bedside into which he stuck his head in the hope of relieving the spasm.

During these years William Burnes, when not teaching Robert and Gilbert himself, and instructing them on the Bible, periodically sent them to different schools to brush up on their work. It shows the remarkable strength and character of this kindly, but stern father that even while trying to eke out an existence for the family and contend with threatening letters from the factor over unpaid rent, he still found the time and inclination to foster the future for his children.

By the age of 18, Robert, a compulsive reader from his earliest days, had devoured the works of Shakespeare, Milton, Dryden, Gray, Shenstone, Pope and Addison. Apart from the fiction of Henry Fielding and Tobias Smollett and the philosophy and history of David Hume and William Robertson, he knew intimately the works of his predecessors in Scottish literature, Allan Ramsay and Robert Fergusson, he read French and had a little Latin. The Bible, as he was to depict in 'The Cotter's Saturday Night', was standard reading for any God-fearing Scottish family. Hardly the background of an 'unlettered ploughman'.

Lochlie

In 1777 Robert's horizons widened immeasurably when his father decided to take the lease of Lochlie Farm, three miles from Mauchline and two and a half miles from Tarbolton. In farming terms, it was little better a bargain than Mount Oliphant, either financially (the rent was high at one pound per acre for each of the 130 acres) or in soil condition. William Burnes had merely exchanged poor, exhausted soil for swampy, undrained land, but for the next four years his family enjoyed a more comfortable lifestyle and Robert found new friends and stimulating company in the nearby farms and villages.

In 1780 the Tarbolton Bachelors' Club was founded and Robert became one of its leading lights, delighting in the debates and gaining confidence from the fierce interchange of passions and personalities. By the following year the poet had become a

Freemason in St David's Lodge, Tarbolton, and it was due to this early masonic commitment that Burns found his later entry into Edinburgh made easier. The ladies had by then also begun to interest him: in his earlier youth the charms of Nellie Kilpatrick and Peggy Thomson had disturbed him, and now at 22 he developed an attachment to Alison Begbie, a farmer's daughter. She turned down his offer of marriage and, depressed and dejected, Burns went off to Irvine to learn the art of flax-dressing. He did set up in business with a partner, but the venture failed. His great friend from the Irvine days was Richard Brown, a sailor and great ladies' man, who, if the stories are to be believed, led Burns astray with his libidinous attitude to women. But more importantly, he was the first person to suggest that Robert become a poet.

On his return to Lochlie early in 1782, Burns found his father involved in litigation with the factor over arrears in rent. The weather had been bad and consequently the harvests poor, and this combined with a general downturn in the economy toppled many small Ayrshire farmers of that period. By the time the sheriff's officers came to the farm to sell their cattle, tools and crops on 17 May 1783, William Burnes was ill with consumption and physically frail after all his years of hard labour. It seems that Burns developed an acute hatred of the landowning classes after years of watching his father being tormented by their factors

making demands for money he could not find: this final seques-
tration of all their goods and chattels strengthened Robert's belief
that all men should share the same rights and privileges. William
Burnes died at Lochlie on 17 February 1784 and was buried in
Alloway Kirkyard, the scene of Tam o' Shanter's nightmare
encounter with the witches.

Mossgiel

Burns's spirit was maybe embittered by life's inequalities, but his
brain was as sharp as ever, and in the autumn of 1783, some five
months before his father's death, he and Gilbert arranged to rent
Mossgiel Farm to provide, as Gilbert later described it, 'an asylum
for the family in case of the worst'. They also shrewdly claimed
against their father's bankrupt estate as employees, and with this
money and whatever savings the family had, after William
Burnes's death, removed to Mossgiel, where Robert became head
of the family. It was at this point that the 'e' was dropped from
their surname. Mossgiel, a 118-acre property with an annual rent
of 90 pounds, lay one mile from Mauchline and, with its heavy
clay soil and high elevation, it was to prove no better a bargain
than the previous farms; even though Robert, determined to make
it a success, voraciously read books on agriculture, attended
markets and searched to find the best seed. However, the
combination of a new-found independence and responsibility as
head of the family seemed to release in him an enormous creative
force. True, he had begun his First Commonplace Book at
Lochlie, in which he jotted down ideas, thoughts and impressions
about life, while he continued to write both poetry and prose.
However, at Mossgiel between the years of 1784 and 1786, he
produced work of such exceptional calibre that had he never
written another word, he would still have been recognized as a
great poet.

The ecclesiastical satires 'Holy Willie's Prayer', 'Address to the
Deil' and 'The Holy Fair', come from this time, as do 'The Twa
Dogs', 'To a Mouse', 'The Jolly Beggars', 'The Cotter's Saturday
Night' and 'Address to the Unco Guid'.

But, apart from this prolific output and the strain of working the farm, Robert also found time for new and influential friends, such as his landlord, Gavin Hamilton, and the lawyer, Robert Aiken of Ayr. John Richmond, one of Gavin Hamilton's clerks, and James Smith, a local draper, together with Burns made up a well-known trio in Mauchline, enjoying many evenings in the Whiteford Inn or Poosie Nansie's. His reputation as a poet was well known locally, but his fame was spreading too amongst 'the Belles of Mauchline'. In May 1785, his first illegitimate child, a daughter, was born to Elizabeth Paton, one of the servants on the farm, and by the end of the same year he had wooed and won Jean Armour; their first set of twins was born the following September. Both these events brought down the wrath of the Kirk Session of Mauchline Parish Church on the poet's head: he had to appear publicly in church to be condemned for the sin of fornication. This was common practice in Scotland at that time, but for Burns it was a bitter humiliation, especially in the case of Jean Armour. After his initial delight at her pregnancy and his written promise of marriage (then recognized as a legal and binding contract), he was shattered to find that Jean's father, totally opposed to the match, had taken steps to have both of their names cut out of the document. Burns's anger and bitterness were reserved for Jean; disgusted by her weakness in handing over the paper to her father, from his viewpoint she had committed an act of betrayal. Jean Armour did become his wife in April 1788; however, it was those very qualities of passive acceptance, which he had despised in her, that gave him so much licence both before and after their marriage. But James Armour, master mason and respected citizen of Mauchline, was not yet finished with the local rhyming rake. In the early summer of 1786, in the knowledge that Burns was in the process of publishing what is now known as the Kilmarnock edition of his poems, he determined to have a financial settlement for Jean and had a warrant issued against the poet for a substantial sum of money. But wily Burns had calculated his actions and had already signed his share of Mossgiel over to Gilbert, ostensibly for the support of Betty Paton's child and included 'the profits that may arise from the publication of my poems presently in the press'.

Burns continued to agonize over Jean and what he saw as her appalling treatment of him, but true to form, in the middle of this turmoil, he turned to Mary Campbell, better known today as

'Highland Mary'. In May of that year he proceeded to offer her marriage, while thinking about emigrating to Jamaica to work as a book-keeper. Whether he was planning to take Mary with him is a matter of conjecture, as is the manner of her death in October of that same year. It was said to be caused by typhus or possibly childbed fever, but there is no certain evidence.

Edinburgh

On 31 July 1786 the Kilmarnock edition of his work was published and in one month the total 612 copies were sold out. Public response was deafening, his poems were read from cottage to castle. The literary world was stunned by the extraordinary talent of this supposed 'unlettered ploughman'. On 3 September Jean Armour gave birth to twins, a boy and girl. Burns left Mossgiel on 27 November for what was to be the first of two winters spent in Edinburgh. It must be remembered that he did not arrive in Edinburgh either friendless, socially inept or intellectually inferior. John Richmond, his friend from Mauchline, now lived there, his masonic affiliations brought many useful contacts, the *literati* fêted him after their 'master' Henry Mackenzie's applause and 'society' drooled over him when the Earl of Glencairn gave his seal of approval. His dress was restrained, his conversation sharp, satirical and decisive, his wit unmatched. His instincts fortunately overruled the often proferred advice to tone down the Scots in his work and, while there is no doubt that he thoroughly enjoyed the fuss he created, in the midst of the social whirl, this well-educated, well-read ploughman, with his feet firmly on the ground, never lost sight of his novelty value. He described his situation in a letter to a friend:

'When proud fortune's ebbing tide recedes' – you may bear me witness, when my bubble of fame was at the highest, I stood, unintoxicated, with the inebriating cup in my hand, looking forward, with rueful resolve, to the hastening time when the stroke of envious Calumny, with all the eagerness of vengeful triumph, should dash it to the ground.
(Letter to Rev. William Greenfield, December 1786)

On the other hand Edinburgh did provide him with convivial company, such as the Crochallan Fencibles, a drinking club of lawyers and merchants, who met regularly at a tavern in Anchor Place. It was here that Burns met Alexander Cunningham, an Edinburgh lawyer, who provied to be a good and loyal friend to him during his lifetime and a great support to Jean Armour after Burns's death. The connections he made in the capital also helped to further his ambition of becoming an excise officer and Patrick Miller, a banker in the city, offered him the lease on Ellisland Farm in Dumfriesshire. Most importantly he saw a second edition of his poems published, a run of some 3000 copies, on 21 April 1787 by William Creech. A notorious skin-flint, Creech cunningly bought the copyright for 100 guineas and managed to hold back payment for sales and subscriptions for another two years. Burns turned down the offer of Ellisland Farm, although he did visit there during his tour of the Borders in May of that year. At this point in his life he saw a return to farming as a regressive step back into back-breaking toil and poverty; he therefore pushed for an excise position, enlisting all the influence he could muster, while friends assured him that a ploughman he was and a ploughman he should stay.

Scottish tours

During the rest of 1787 Burns travelled quite extensively through Scotland. Apart from his Borders tour, in June he travelled to Argyll to the west Highlands and in August he began a three-week journey around the Highlands with his friend William Nicol, staying with the Duke and Duchess of Athole at Blair Castle, dining at Castle Gordon at Fochabers, visiting Culloden Moor, the scene of the last Jacobite stand, and the site of the Battle of Bannockburn. In October, in the company of Dr James Adair, Burns travelled through Stirling on the way to Harvieston in Clackmananshire to stay with the Chalmers family. Relatives of Gavin Hamilton, Burns had met and admired their daughter Peggy before, and he now proposed marriage to her but was turned down.

Meanwhile, in July of that same year, between his travels he had returned to Mossgiel and found James Armour with an entirely different view of him. Now that the father of Jean's twins was a famous, celebrated and, he assumed, soon to be wealthy poet, he was a decidedly different catch from the unsuccessful farmer and local scribbler that Jean's father had previously refused. Still bitter about her, Burns reluctantly visited Jean and their children and, by the following March, she had produced their second set of twins. Sadly both children died within a few weeks of their birth.

Dumfriesshire

The 'Clarinda' episode from December 1787 until the following spring is a curious hiatus in Burns's life, apart from the now famous, passionate correspondence between them and the beautiful love song 'Ae Fond Kiss', it appears to have suspended him from reality for a time.

Burns signed the lease on Ellisland Farm in Dumfriesshire on 18 March and, by the end of April, he and Jean Armour were married by mutual declaration. He still pursued an excise post as a safeguard against the failure of the farm and in July he was issued with a commission, although he did not receive an appointment until September 1789. With it came a salary of 50 pounds per annum. In June he moved to Ellisland to organize the building of a farmhouse, Jean remaining at Mauchline with their only son, his twin sister having died the previous year. They joined Burns at Christmas, living in a cottage until the farmhouse was finally finished the following summer. Ellisland stands beside the River Nith, six miles north of the town of Dumfries and, with its exhausted, undrained, unfertilized soil and a rent of 70 pounds per year, it was certainly a poor investment. However, for the next three years Burns lived there with Jean and their growing brood of children, combining the arduous toil of working an unproductive farm with his excise post. It was with great relief that he managed to extricate himself from the Ellisland lease, and, in November 1791, the family moved into a flat in Stinking Vennel in Dumfries, remaining there until May 1793, when they found a red sandstone house in

Ellisland Farm

Mill Vennel (now Burns Street), where the poet died three years later. In Dumfries Burns concentrated his efforts on his excise work and, despite his outbursts of republican sympathy for the French Revolution, he was a valued officer, often commended and subsequently promoted.

During the Dumfriesshire years, in spite of the workload, ill-health and the cares of a growing family, Burns never lost his eye for the 'fairer sex'. Anna Park, the barmaid at the Globe Inn in Dumfries, gave birth to his daughter in March 1791, after which Jean, in her usual docile way, took the child into her home and brought her up as one of her own. Jean Lorimer, the daughter of a local farmer, inspired his 'Chloris' songs and the beautiful and bright Maria Riddell filled a void in his life both intellectually and emotionally. He continued to correspond with Mrs Dunlop of Dunlop, a motherly figure, who began writing to him after reading the Kilmarnock volume of his poems. His relations with these last two ladies were unfortunately marred for a time because of his headstrong behaviour. In Maria Riddell's case the cause of the breach was the so-called 'rape of the Sabine women' incident and he bitterly offended Mrs Dunlop, knowing two of her daughters were married to exiled French royalists, when he described Louis XVI and Marie Antionette as 'a perjured blockhead and an unprincipled prostitute'. Maria Riddell regretted their estrangement and it was she who instigated the truce between them, but the divide that separated Burns and Mrs Dunlop was only mended on his death-bed, when he finally received a reply to his contrite letters. Agnes McLehose briefly entered his life once more in 1791, when she contacted him to ask for help for a servant girl, who had given birth to his son after he left Edinburgh, and only a few months before his death he was writing tributes to his nurse Jessie Lewars, the sister of a fellow excise officer. Jean Armour bore him nine children, made him a home and tolerated his extra-marital activities, in the knowledge that she would rather live with him than live without him. Burns loved his children deeply and was always concerned for their future welfare. Jean he loved in his own way, but she could share only part of his life, that of hearth and home, while he needed stimulus, both socially and intellectually, to help absorb the energies of his boiling brain.

In later life Burns's artistic talents were devoted almost exclusively to Scottish song, saving many lyrics and melodies, which would otherwise have been lost for ever. From 1788 until 1792 he wrote, rearranged and compiled songs for James Johnson's *Scots Musical Museum*, later performing the same task from 1792 until his death in 1796 for George Thomson's *Select Scottish Airs*. The debt we owe to him for this service is immeasurable, considering his other responsibilities, his poor health and the fact that the work was totally unpaid.

Burns's health, dogged throughout his life by depressions, melancholia and a heart condition, took a severe downturn in the last six months of his life. In addition to these old agues, he developed joint pains and so-called 'rheumatic' fevers. He did not die from alcoholism, as has often been suggested. His doctor misdiagnosed his final illness as 'flying gout' and undoubtedly hastened his end by sending him to bathe in the freezing waters of the Solway Firth.

Unable to work in the last months, he was seriously worried about his finances and his family's future welfare if he died. Acute shortages of food during the winter of 1795–6 caused hardship all over the country and by February and March there were riots in the streets of Dumfries. Having managed to live within his income during his lifetime, it must have hurt his pride that in the final weeks he was reduced to asking friends to repay money he had loaned and begging others for financial assistance to pay small accounts.

His fears for Jean and the children proved unfounded, due to the unstinting work of his friends, Alexander Cunningham and John Syme. They collected a substantial sum of money through public subscription and from the sales of his work to ensure a comfortable and secure lifestyle for the family. Robert Burns died, aged 37, on 21 July 1796, and was buried on 25 July in St Michael's Churchyard, Dumfries. Jean, absent from the funeral as she was giving birth to their youngest child, outlived him by 38 years, dying in 1834 at the age of 67.

We will probably never fully appreciate Burns's contribution to Scottish literature and to Scotland. In a nation feeling its roots slipping away, he kept the flame of patriotism burning. He translated into poetry the certainties of life in their simplest terms, good and bad, and made a celebration of them. In less able hands the sentimentalism in his work might have appeared facile, but Burns was not a 'heaven-taught ploughman', but an educated and skilled craftsman in the arts of poetry and song.

Robert Burns was no stranger to the gloomier side of 'man's estate', having many period of black despair, but in the midst of his pain he recognized that there were always moments, no matter how fleeting, when the spirits were lifted and the mind reassured. In his finest work he catches these moments and shares them with us. His words have the power to touch the heart and linger long after the touching.

The History
of the Burns Supper

The tradition of the Burns Supper in recognition and celebration of the poet's life and work began in the early years after his death. The first recorded supper occurred in Ayrshire in the summer of 1801, although others are believed to have taken place earlier. Held in Burns Cottage in Alloway (then an inn), the party consisted of nine of Burns's closest friends, including Robert Aiken, the eloquent lawyer, and John Ballantine, the provost of Ayr. The speech was given by the Reverend Hamilton Paul and, even here at the first recorded dinner, haggis was served. It was decided at this meeting that the following year's gathering should take place on the poet's birthday in January and because of a mistake in Currie's biography of Burns (corrected some years later) this was thought to be 29 January. Over the next ten years the date for the dinners shifted between winter and summer, but eventually, due to pressure of work in the farming community during the summer months, it was decided that January was the most suitable time.

It is difficult to date when this steadily growing circle actually became the Alloway Burns Club, but by the end of the first decade of the 19th century they were certainly known as such. During the early years other Burns clubs sprung up in Greenock, Paisley and Kilmarnock and, helped by increasing press coverage, word of these events soon spread until the original concept of a dinner commemorating the poet was taken up by groups of individuals and clubs who added a Burns Supper to their yearly programme. By 1830 these gatherings were widespread, not just in Ayrshire and Dumfriesshire, where Burns had lived, but all over the country. These clubs, although run on an informal basis, were the forerunners of the official Burns clubs of today. The parent body of this world-wide association is the Burns Federation, based in Kilmarnock, which at present lists 300–400 affiliated clubs and between 200 and 300 individuals as active federation members.

There is an important distinction between a Burns Supper and the Burns Anniversary Dinner given by Burns clubs. Club Anniversary Dinners have the early format of speeches, music and song, 'The Immortal Memory' being the high point of an evening dedicated to Burns's life and work. Burns Suppers follow this style, but some are on a looser framework and some end the evening with a dance. Needless to say, traditionalists frown on this addition to the event, but it is certainly one way of introducing younger generations to a Burns Supper and the poet's work.

There are also those who disapprove of a female presence at Burns Suppers, some clubs still will not allow it, which seems at odds with Burns's own life and ignores the fact that a lady (Primrose Kennedy of Drumellan) attended the first dinner in Alloway. The 'lasses', however, have occasionally got their own back. In 1920, in Shotts in Lanarkshire, the first all-ladies' club was founded; there was in fact quite a spate of these all-ladies' clubs in the district at that time. The Burns Federation itself has, to date, had four women presidents. The first, in 1970, was Jane Burgoyne, an Edinburgh teacher.

With further regard to the fairer sex, the 'Toast to the Lasses' has also undergone a change from earlier days. Originally it was a thank you to the ladies for supplying the food for the evening, by way of a salute to them for their kindness. It did not take the form it does now, whereby the 'lasses' are lambasted for their failings, before being praised for their attributes. In the earlier speeches, too, the only ladies mentioned were those in Burns's life. At 'Bachelor' Suppers, a gentleman delivers 'The Reply' on behalf of the 'lasses'.

The most atmospheric of all Burns Suppers is said to take place in the Globe Inn in Dumfries. A regular haunt of the poet, so strong is the memory of him that, to quote Mr Ogilvie, past president of the Dumfries Burns Club, 'should the spirit of Burns appear at the table, no one would be surprised'. Certainly the inn has the feeling that time has passed it by, particularly in a room upstairs where Burns scratched some lines on the window and nothing feels as if it has changed for centuries. The Dumfries Burns Club itself was not founded until 1820, although the previour year's celebrations to mark the poet's birthday had been held at the inn.

It was during the earlier dinner in 1819 that the decision was taken to order from Spode, a porcelain punch bowl to be used on all future occasions. It came with a silver ladle, mugs and three dozen glasses. Decorated with Burns's portrait surrounded by depictions of the important places in his life, the centre of the bowl has a painting of the Mausoleum in Dumfries; thistles, leaves and fruit are intertwined throughout and on the bottom rim there are replicas of the signatures of the group of his friends who commissioned the bowl. It can be seen today along with other Burns memorabilia in the Robert Burns Centre in Dumfries.

The Globe Inn, Dumfries

The Basic Elements
of a
Burns Supper

The Burns Supper exists as a celebration of the art and endeavour of the poet. But the underlying objective and ultimately the best test of a successful evening is how many of the guests have their love of Burns rekindled and how many others go home determined to read him for the first time. The event should not be just a celebration, with all the pleasure that this entails, it should also act as a reaffirmation of the humanitarian values enshrined in his work.

The order of events

Whether a Burns Supper is organized by a Burns Club, any other club or a group of friends, the basic format is the same. After the Chairman for the evening has welcomed the company, a recitation of 'The Selkirk Grace' follows. Dinner is served, including the piping-in of the haggis and then a rendering of Burns's 'Address to the Haggis'. After the meal is finished, the principal speaker is called upon to deliver the main speech of the evening 'The Immortal Memory'. This is followed by a short appreciation of his efforts and the two other compulsory speeches, 'The Toast to the Lasses' and 'The Reply'. Other speeches can be included: the Ayr Burns Club always has a toast to 'Auld Ayr'. Songs and recitations follow the speeches and the evening is brought to a close by the singing of 'Auld Lang Syne'.

The evening can thus be broken up into three main sections: the Dinner, the Speeches, and the Songs and Recitations.

The DINNER

1 The Chairman welcomes the company.
2 The clergyman recites 'The Selkirk Grace'.
3 Dinner is served including the piping-in of the haggis and a rendering of Burns's 'To a Haggis'.
4 The Chairman proposes 'The Loyal Toast'.
5 The club Secretary makes any announcements about future events and plans.

The SPEECHES

1 The principal speaker is called upon to deliver 'The Immortal Memory'.
2 A short speech in appreciation of the speaker's efforts is given.
3 'The Toast to the Lasses' is proposed by a gentleman speaker.
4 'The Reply' from a lady speaker follows.
5 Other speeches and toasts can now be added.

The SONGS and RECITATIONS

1 Various songs and recitations of Burns's work.
2 The evening ends with the company singing 'Auld Lang Syne'.

As a guideline the proceedings should last from 6.30 pm until 11.00 pm.

Where to begin

When considering arranging a Burns Supper, first contact your local Burns Club or the Burns Federation in Kilmarnock for help. Your local club will be able to give advice, perhaps suggest speakers and tell you of other Burns Suppers in the area which might clash with the evening you have chosen.

The date

A Burns Supper does not have to take place on 25 January, it can be given any time in the weeks preceding or following the anniversary of the poet's birth. It will also be easier to find good speakers if you are prepared to move further away from the actual date.

The organizer

The first task in front of anyone planning a Burns Supper is to delegate an organizer, preferably with a few able helpers. In the official Burns clubs the duty of organizer usually falls to the Secretary, who can enlist the aid of two or three committee members. Other clubs deciding to add a Burns Supper to their diary of events should follow the same guidelines. For those daring enough to attempt a dinner in their own home, the bulk of the responsibility must rest on their own shoulders.

The Chairman

After the organizer is chosen, a Chairman must be appointed for the evening. Normally, but not necessarily, this role falls to the club President. Whoever takes on the task should be adept at and have experience of guiding an evening from the introductory speech through to the final farewell. It requires a commanding, but genial host, preferably someone with a love of Burns, who can keep control of the arrangements, especially the timing, introduce the performers and speakers and at the beginning be able to set a warm, inspiring tone for the evening ahead.

The essential ingredients for the festivities are as follows:
1 A clergyman to deliver 'The Selkirk Grace'.
2 A piper to pipe in the haggis or perhaps a fiddler (it has been done).

3   A speaker for the principal speech of the evening 'The Immortal Memory'.
4   A speaker for 'The Toast to the Lasses'.
5   A lady to deliver 'The Reply'.
6   Two or three speakers to deliver recitations of Burns's poems.
7   A male and female vocalist for Burns's songs.
8   An accompanist for the vocalists, pianist or fiddler or both.

How to Organize a
Burns Supper

The hotel

Anyone undertaking this enterprise should begin arrangements as soon as possible. It is never too early to book the hotel, speakers, singers, accompanists and the piper. Inspect a few hotels; most will have had some experience of catering for a Burns Supper, whether large or small scale. Ask for a quotation from each, for the cost of the function suite, including a separate reception room for the top-table guests, dinner and any drinks served as part of the proceedings. Most good hotels will be able to offer various menus for a Burns Supper and be prepared to negotiate prices. Haggis does not have to be the main course, it can be served as a replacement for the traditional fish course. Details you will need for the manager are: the approximate length of the evening (is there to be a dance after the dinner and speeches?), how formal the style, and a rough idea of numbers. At this stage you should also discuss various dates available at the hotels before contacting the speakers.

Speakers

The principal speech is 'The Immortal Memory' and whoever delivers this is largely responsible for the success of the evening. Contact your local Burns Club or the Burns Federation about finding a good speaker (the best are often booked years ahead) and ask friends and colleagues from other clubs and societies to recommend their past successes. Once a speaker has been decided upon, after a meeting to assess his talents or better still having listened to him speak, the club Secretary should then write inviting him to speak, remembering the greater his reputation the sooner you will have to try. If an agreement is reached and a date fixed, you should, even at this early stage, give him a brief résumé of your club, its history and an outline of the tone, style and hopes you have for your dinner. The other speakers who deliver 'The Toast to the Lasses' and 'The Reply' are invited to take part some six to eight months before the event. In many Burns clubs these two speakers can be found amongst the members. At a later time it would be a good idea to put the speakers in touch with one another and avoid any duplication of material. It should be agreed at an early stage just how long each speech will last. 'The Immortal Memory' should last approximately 30 minutes and the other two speeches a maximum of ten minutes each. It is customary that an invitation to speak includes a supper invitation for the speaker's partner.

The clergyman, singers, accompanists, readers and the piper

The clergyman, singers, accompanists, readers and the piper are also invited guests at the feast. They should be contacted as soon as possible and their part in the evening's entertainment explained. Most will have experience of Burns Suppers and will know exactly what is expected of them.

Fees

The question of fees for speakers and performers rarely arises within Burns club circles, only occasional travelling expenses being necessary, but in the larger world professional speakers and performers would normally be paid for their services.

Follow-up plans

Once the arrangements for speakers, performers and hotel have been agreed and confirmed in writing, they should be contacted

Bill o' Fare

'Some hae meat and canna eat
And some wad eat that want it:
But we hae meat and we can eat,
And sae the Lord be thankit.'

Cock-a-Leekie

★

Haggis,

warm, reekin, rich wi'
Champit Tatties, Bashed Neeps

Address to the Haggis
Mr A. McPherson

Steak Pie

Tipsy Laird

A Tassie o' Coffee

TOAST LIST

Grace .... Rev. D. Ness
The Queen .... The Chairman
Greetings from
  Kindred Clubs .... Hon. Secretary

THE IMMORTAL MEMORY

Mr Tom Raffel

Song .... Miss Ann Maclachlan

Auld Ayr .... Mr Philip Craig

Reading .... Mrs Jeanette Service

Reply .... Provost Daniel McNeill

Song .... Mr David Boyd

Reading .... Mrs Jeanette Service

The Lassies .... Rev. David Ness

Song .... Miss Ann Maclachlan

Reply .... Rev. Effie Campbell

Song .... Mr David Boyd

Vote of Thanks .... Mrs Roma Ferguson

Accompanist .... Mrs Jean Kean

Piper .... Mr John Paton

———

A typical evening's programme of the Ayr Burns Club

again in early December to remind them of their commitments. By this time whoever is to deliver 'The Immortal Memory' will have a basic speech plan prepared. At this juncture the Secretary, Chairman and a few committee members from the club should meet the speaker for a final briefing. This should be an opportunity for all views to be aired and any misunderstandings that might have occurred to be cleared up. The speaker should be reminded of the club's aspirations for the evening, given details of the level of formality, the length of the proceedings, how long he is expected to speak (remember 30 minutes is the average) whether there will be any distinguished guests and the total number expected to attend. Moreover, this is the time to ask someone from the club to prepare an alternative speech, should the speaker become ill or be unable to attend at the last minute.

Dress

Everyone involved in the evening will need to be advised about dress. At a Burns Club Anniversary Dinner, guests at the top table wear evening dress, some Highland dress, while the other guests dress informally. This is a good rule to follow, but there is nothing to prevent the other guests wearing evening dress if they choose, and at some large formal dinners it is compulsory for all. It is often requested that everyone wear an item of tartan.

Invitations, tickets, programmes

Invitations to the dinner are issued by the club Secretary. Apart from the speakers and performers, local dignitaries are usually included. Within the Burns club circle this honour would also be extended to members of the Burns Federation. Tickets are sold to members, friends and visitors and there is no maximum or minimum number for a Burns Supper. Before working out a ticket price you must take all the expenses into consideration (ie the cost of dinner plus the hiring of the function suite, any expenses incurred by speakers or performers, printer's costs, postage and any miscellaneous outgoings). Tickets and programmes do have to be printed, but perhaps the costs could be reduced if you are fortunate enough to have a printer within the club or society. The programme includes the menu, or bill of fare as it is called and a list of the speeches, speakers and performers. Both tickets and programmes should be on good quality card and boldly printed. A programme for each guest, to keep as a memento of the occasion, should be displayed on the table.

Seating plans

The top-table party consists of the Chairman, the speakers, the minister, other specially invited guests and local dignitaries along with their respective husbands and wives. They gather in a separate reception room for drinks before the evening begins. A seating plan should be on display in this room as the party must be arranged in order before leaving to be piped into the main dining room.

Top Table Plan	
1 Invited guest	6 The Chairman
2 Husband/wife of speaker	7 Husband/wife of speaker
3 Speaker – 'The Toast to the Lasses'	8 The Minister
4 Husband/wife of speaker	9 Speaker – 'The Reply'
5 Speaker – 'The Immortal Memory'	10 Club Secretary
	11 Husband/wife of speaker
	12 Invited guest

It is the job of the Secretary to ensure that the party are formed into a procession and arrive at the table in the order shown on the plan. Decisions on the table placings are taken by the Secretary and Chairman together. There is no set order to be followed, it is merely a matter of personal choice and discretion. The only exception to this is that the proposer of 'The Immortal Memory' sits on the Chairman's right-hand side. A table plan is also needed for all the other guests at the Supper, ensuring the company is well mixed, with committee members and any other specially invited guests spread throughout. There will always be last-minute alterations in the seating plan due to illness or cancellations. Consult the hotel manager and his staff, they will know best how to rearrange the numbers and tables.

The final arrangements

A week before the event visit the hotel once more and discuss with the manager any details that either of you may have overlooked. This will give you another chance to see the function suite (it may not be quite as you remember), double check the table layout, menu and drinks facilities and seating arrangements, making sure that there is space for the piper to reach the top table (the piper and procession will move clockwise round the room to the seats). On the day itself visit the hotel to inspect the tables, make any change of seating and deliver the programmes. In the evening, once the guests have arrived and had drinks, the Secretary and a few committee members can ensure everyone finds their allotted seat on the plan.

The press

A short press release should be sent to the local newspaper, with notes on speakers and performers. If the event is not covered by a reporter (this can be averted by sending an invitation to the local newspaper editor), an account of the proceedings should be delivered the following day.

The Dinner

Some hae meat and canna eat
And some wad eat that want it:
But we hae meat and we can eat,
And sae the Lord be thankit.
(*The Selkirk Grace*)

Recitation of 'The Selkirk Grace'

Once the company are in their places the piper proceeds to lead in the top-table guests. The assembly is signalled to stand and begins a handclap, while the procession moves clockwise around the room to their seats. As soon as everyone is seated, the Chairman will rise to make a short speech of welcome. This lasts only a few minutes and sets a convivial tone for the evening ahead. In addition to the printed programme he will have a more detailed list of speakers and performers and, during the rest of the evening, before introducing each speaker, he will deliver a short preamble on his or her background, including anything relevant to Burns and his work. After the welcome, grace is said, either by a clergyman or the Chairman himself. 'The Selkirk Grace' is normally chosen and the story behind its association with Burns is an interesting one.

During his tour of Galloway in 1794, Burns and his friend, John Syme, stayed for a few days with the Earl of Selkirk at St Mary's Isle, Kirkcudbright, the Selkirks' family home. The visit was a huge success with Burns at his very best, impressing his host and the other guests with his erudite wit and stimulating conversation. When asked to say the blessing before dinner he recited an old Scots grace, which he altered slightly. It thereafter become known as 'The Selkirk Grace'.

Dinner is then served. Cock-a-leekie soup is the standard first course. This is followed by the haggis with champit tatties and bashed neeps (mashed potatoes and mashed turnip). Today haggis is synonymous with Burns Night. No longer regularly made in Scottish households, as it was in the poet's lifetime, it has assumed a kind of magical significance on 25 January and is itself almost an honorary guest at the feast. The 'slaying' of the haggis is a vital part of the evening's ritual, probably more famous than many of the other ingredients of the Burns Supper.

The haggis ceremony

The haggis ceremony begins when the Chairman is signalled from the kitchen that all is ready. He asks the company to stand to receive the haggis and the piper or fiddler then leads in the chef carrying the haggis aloft, followed by a third person with two bottles of whisky. They march around the room to the top table, while the guests perform a slow handclap. The platter is placed on the table in front of the Chairman, who invites the chef and piper to join him in a glass of whisky to toast the haggis. Together they raise their glasses in the Gaelic toast '*Slainte mhath*' (pronounced 'slan-je-va') – your good health. The chef and piper then leave the proceedings (the piper rejoining his table) and the company take their seats. The Chairman or an invited guest then recites 'To a Haggis'.

To a Haggis

Fair fa' your honest, sonsie face	*good luck to – jolly*
Great Chieftain o' the Puddin-race!	
Aboon them a' ye tak your place,	*above*
Painch, tripe, or thairm:	*paunch – intestines*
Weel are ye wordy o' a grace	*worthy*
As lang's my arm.	

The groaning trencher there ye fill,
Your hurdies like a distant hill, *buttocks*
Your pin wad help to mend a mill *would*
In time o' need,
While thro' your pores the dews distil
Like amber bead.

His knife see Rustic-labour dight, *clean, wipe*
An' cut you up wi' ready sleight,
Trenching your gushing entrails bright
Like onie ditch; *any*
And then, O what a glorious sight,
Warm-reekin, rich! *steaming*

Then, horn for horn they stretch *horn – spoon*
 an' strive,
Deil tak the hindmost, on they drive, *last*
Till a' their weel-swall'd
 kytes belyve *swelled stomachs by-and-by*
Are bent like drums;
Then auld Guidman, maist like to *almost –*
 rive, *burst*
'Bethankit' hums. *murmurs 'God be thanked'*

Is there that owre his French *ragout*, *over*
Or *olio* that wad staw a sow, *would surfeit*
O *fricassee* wad mak her spew
Wi' perfect sconner, *disgust*
Looks down wi' sneering, scornfu' view
On sic a dinner?

Poor devil! see him ower his trash,
As feckless as a wither'd rash, *feeble – rush*
His spindle shank a guid whip-lash, *thin leg – good*
His nieve a nit; *clost fist – nut*
Thro' bluidy flood or field to dash, *bloody*
O how unfit!

But mark the Rustic, haggis-fed,
The trembling earth resounds his tread;
Clap in his walie nieve a blade,   *large fist*
He'll mak it whissle;   *whistle*
An' legs, an' arms, an' heads will sned   *lop off*
Like taps o' thrissle.   *tops of thistles*

Ye Pow'rs wha mak mankind your care
And dish them out their bill o' fare,
Auld Scotland wants nae skinking ware   *thin stuff*
That jaups in luggies;   *splashes in bowls*
But if ye wish her gratefu' prayer,
Gie her a Haggis!   *Give*

The poem can be read, but the spectacle looks and sounds better if the words are memorized and delivered with enthusiasm. A knife should already be to hand on the table and as the speaker reaches the line, 'An' cut you up wi' ready sleight', he slits open the haggis. If the haggis has been cooked in the traditional manner, it will be encased in animal intestine and as such is difficult to cut. To avoid any embarrassment on the part of the speaker, ensure that a sharp pointed knife is supplied. There are many different ways to perform this operation, but bear in mind that the object of the exercise is to be able to spoon out the contents on to the waiting plates. It is customary to applaud when the speaker finishes the address and at some Burns Suppers the company stands to toast the haggis with a glass of whisky. Although frowned upon by purists, in some clubs and at many Burns Suppers today, haggis is no longer the main course. Instead it appears on the menu in place of the fish course. Beef or turkey are popular main-course choices, and are especially welcomed by those who have not quite attained the superlative palate of the seasoned haggis connoisseur. Tipsy Laird, or sherry trifle as it is better known, is one of the most favoured puddings, but others are equally acceptable. A Scottish cheese served with oatcakes follows or coffee can be served directly after the pudding.

'The Loyal Toast'

Once dinner is over, this section of the evening is brought to a close by the Chairman asking the company to stand and drink a toast to the health of the monarch.

Club announcements

In Burns clubs this is the time for the Secretary to read out any messages of goodwill from other clubs and make announcements about club events or future plans.

Bill o' Fare

COCK-A-LEEKIE SOUP

Ingredients:

1 boiling fowl ($2^1/_2$–$3^1/_2$ lbs) giblets	1 bouquet garni
4 pints water	8 prunes (soaked overnight)
6 leeks, cleaned and sliced	salt and pepper

Method
Put the fowl and giblets into a large pan and cover with water. Add leeks, bouquet garni and seasonings. Bring to the boil, skim the surface, cover and simmer for 2¹/₂ hours or until the bird is tender. Remove the fowl, disgard giblets and bouquet garni, skim any fat from the surface. Add prunes, cook for a further 30 minutes, check seasonings and serve. The chicken can be used as a separate course or served cold later.

Serves 6–8.

THE HAGGIS

Most haggis eaten nowadays is commercially prepared, whereas in the past it was produced at home from everyday cheap cuts of meat combined with oatmeal, onion, seasonings and beef suet, the whole minced and sewn up in a sheep's stomach before being boiled for three hours. The traditional recipe is as follows.

Ingredients:

1 sheep's stomach bag	8 oz/277 gm oatmeal
2 onions	(pinhead)
1 sheep's pluck (heart, lights	1 teaspoon ground black
and liver)	pepper
1 tablespoon salt	8 oz/227 gm beef suet
	stock or gravy

Method
Clean the stomach bag by washing thoroughly, turn inside out, scald and scrape with a knife. Soak overnight in cold salted water. Wash the pluck well, place in a large saucepan of cold water and bring to the boil. Hang the windpipe over the side of the pan. Boil for two hours, remove (reserve liquid) and mince the heart and lights and grate the liver. Put all the meat into a bowl, add onions (finely chopped), oatmeal (toasted in the oven), suet and seasonings. Mix and add enough of the cooking liquid or fresh stock to moisten the mixture well. Fill the stomach bag slightly over half full and sew it up with strong thread. Prick the skin in a few places to prevent it bursting during cooking. Sit the haggis on a metal plate in a saucepan of boiling water (enough to cover the haggis) and boil for

three hours, without lid. Keep adding boiling water to keep haggis covered.

Serve with mashed potatoes and mashed turnip.

Ready-made haggis from butchers and supermarkets can be reheated (since it is already cooked) in one of two ways. Either place in a casserole with a little water in a moderate oven or heat in a good amount of water in a pot on top of the stove. Both methods require cooking for $^1/_2$–$^3/_4$ hr per lb and the haggis should always be wrapped in foil. It must be thoroughly heated and served as hot as possible, with mashed turnip and potatoes. For some, haggis is an acquired taste, but nevertheless it is eaten regularly in many parts of the world (including Scotland), not just at Burns Suppers or on St Andrews Night, but as a customary part of the diet. Today haggis consumption is actually increasing and for those who no longer eat meat, some butchers now produce a vegetarian alternative. Butchers can supply haggis in either the natural skin or a plastic covering, the only benefit to be gained from the artificial one, if ordering by post, is that it keeps better. Size is variable: from as small as 12 oz up to 4 lb.

TYPSY LAIRD (Sherry Trifle)

Ingredients:

1 Victoria sponge cake (cut into slices)

$^3/_4$ lb (12 oz) raspberry jam

1 wine glass of sherry

2 tablespoons brandy or if preferred Drambuie

Home-made egg custard (see below)

$^3/_4$ lb (12 oz) raspberries

2 bananas (optional)

$^1/_2$ pint (300 ml) double cream

1 tablespoon caster sugar

Toasted almonds

Custard:

8 fl oz (250 ml) milk

5 fl oz (150 ml) double cream

2 egg yolks

1 oz (50 gm) caster sugar

Few drops of vanilla essence

Method

Place the sponge in the base of a large glass bowl and spread with the raspberry jam. Mix the sherry and brandy and sprinkle evenly over the sponge allowing it to soak in. Next add a layer of raspberries and sliced bananas.

To make the custard, whisk together the egg yolks, sugar and vanilla essence until pale and creamy. Heat the milk and cream together in a saucepan until boiling point then stir into the egg mixture. Once it is well blended, return to the pan and stir continuously over a low heat until the custard thickens. Pour into a dish and allow to cool. When quite cool, pour the custard over the layer of fruit, spreading evenly. Next whip the double cream, add sugar to sweeten and spoon on top of custard. Decorate with toasted almonds.

Serves 6–8.

CHEESES

Any Scottish cheese is suitable for Burns Night. Some of the better known are Scottish Cheddar, crowdie, Caboc and Islay Dunlop.

The
Immortal Memory Speech

Where to begin

After dinner there is a break in the proceedings for approximately 15 minutes. The company then return to their seats and the atmosphere is prepared for the second part of the evening, sometimes by a song or a tune on the fiddle. This paves the way for the Chairman to introduce the principal speaker and the high point of the evening: 'The Immortal Memory' speech. The Chairman should give a brief resume of the speaker's life and interests, particularly those points associated with Burns and his work; any books written, speeches made or simply his love of Burns.

There are many different types of 'Immortal Memory' speech, from the light-hearted to the literary, but they all have one aim in common: they should make everyone in the room want to go home and read Burns. How is this achieved and in the space of 30 minutes?

If you have been asked to deliver the speech, the following points could be of some help. Think of the sentiments in 'Auld Lang Syne', this will give you the key to the speech. Concentrate on what we owe Burns, his hopes for humanity and his love of his country. Through Burns's work and your interpretation of it you should aim to touch the hearts and minds of the audience. Life's experiences in all its extremities are felt by everyone and the common ground between you, your audience and Robert Burns is to be found in these events. You should evoke memories in the listeners' minds of moments when they shared the same feelings or survived the same trials as Burns. A good speech creates a bond with Burns, to give courage and inspiration by illuminating how he perceived, and came to terms with, life's joys and sorrows. Through Burns, the audience should learn more about themselves, their fellow Scots and their fellow human beings in general.

Burns as a Scotsman is an important part of the speech, especially to those expatriot Scots at dinners abroad, but avoid being too narrowly nationalistic and try to introduce a universal feel to the speech. Do this and you will have achieved your own and the poet's aims.

> Then let us pray that come it may, –
> As come it will for a' that –
> That Sense and Worth, o'er a' the earth,
> May bear the gree, and a' that.   *supremacy*
> For a' that, and a' that,
> It's comin' yet for a' that,
> That Man to Man, the world o'er,
> Shall brothers be for a' that!
> (*A Man's a Man for a' That*)

In the audience will be some who have never read Burns, you should make them feel that they have stumbled upon an important part of their personal heritage. On the other hand those who already know Burns should feel gratified by the remembrance of things forgotten.

Again, remember 'Auld Lang Syne'. These suppers have continued down through the years. They help to keep the spirit of Burns alive and tonight you are a link in that chain. 'Kindred clubs' is one of the toasts at a supper, but kindred spirits best describes those who feel a harmony with Burns, in his pain, his passion and his warmth.

For many, the Burns Supper means a splendid night out in convivial company which comes along every January to brighten up the long winter months. But for the great majority, it is a night spent in the fellowship of Burns, a night of remembrance of the poet's life and work and a night to consider one's own life. The evening should rejuvenate, not just Burns's memory, but each individual's spirit and it should be looked back on as a joyous, shared experience.

It helps to read as many of the best biographies (see the bibliography at the back of this book) as possible, along with books on Ayrshire, Dumfriesshire and Scotland in general, but, before all, read Burns's works, which are the finest examples of communication you could ever wish to follow.

In the following pages you will find a choice of themes for 'The Immortal Memory' speech. Each of these examines a certain feature of Burns's life and work. After introducing the theme, you can begin with a text to emphasize this feature, developing your speech around it, using quotes from Burns and others if necessary. You can mention other poets and writers, but do little more than touch on them. You should take into consideration the club or gathering that you are addressing (ie what their wishes may be for the evening and how you can relate Burns's life and work to them). Finish by summing up, perhaps giving a new focus on the theme.

It is never a bad thing to 'try out' your speech on one or two friends before the event itself. Public speaking is now much less practised than of old and practice makes perfect: also it lets you check the time that the speech may be expected to last.

At the end of the speech you should ask the company to rise and drink a toast to 'The Immortal Memory of Robert Burns'.

Suggested themes for
'The Immortal Memory' speech

Burns's life

Anyone being asked to deliver 'The Immortal Memory' for the first time automatically thinks of the speech in terms of Burns's life. You will see from the following selection of topics that a detailed examination of Burns's life from birth to death is not essential. Rather, to keep your audience's attention and hopefully encourage their interest in Burns, try to look at the circumstances of his life from an unusual angle. It could, for example, be split into two stages: that is, after Edinburgh and at the end of his days in Dumfries. You could also ponder on what might have been Burns's thoughts at these times.

Although written years earlier, the last two verses of 'To a Mouse' sum up what must have been his feelings as he returned to the farmer's life after the heady days and raised hopes of Edinburgh:

> But Mousie, thou art no thy lane,   *not alone*
> In proving foresight may be vain:
> The best-laid schemes o' Mice an' Men
> Gang aft a-gley,   *go often wrong*
> An' lea'e us nought but grief and pain,   *leave*
> For promis'd joy.
>
> Still thou art blest, compar'd wi' me!
> The present only toucheth thee:
> But, Och! I backward cast my e'e,
> On prospects drear!
> An' forward, tho' I canna see,
> I guess an' fear!

As a further help, a selection of quotations is given at the back of the book.

INTRODUCTION: *The Ayrshire background*

Until the Kilmarnock edition of his poems was published and he started on the road to fame, but sadly not fortune, Robert Burns led a largely isolated life in Ayrshire. There, he 'first committed the sin of ryhme' at the age of 15 and there also, some ten years later, he began composing the works which made his reputation and ensured his place in literary history. You could at this point give a short description of the working conditions of an Ayrshire farmer at that time, emphasizing Burns's great achievements both physical and literary. But even in difficult days, Burns always found cause to smile, whether in mirth at his fellow man, in companionship with the animals who shared his burdens, or simply at the sheer joy of being alive.

> The honest heart that's free frae a'
> Intended fraud or guile,
> However Fortune kick the ba',   *ball*
> Has ay some cause to smile;
> (*Epistle to Davie*)

DEVELOPMENT: *After Edinburgh*

By the end of 1786 the Ayrshire farmer had become the toast of Edinburgh and although enjoying the excitement he caused, Burns was not fooled by the adoration. He did hope that he might live by the power of his pen and abandon the rigours of farming, but any contacts he made proved to be unfruitful and most felt that the 'ploughman poet' should fulfil his role in life and return to the soil. By the end of the second winter in the capital, his fate was sealed. He brought the affair with Clarinda to a close, accepted the farm at Ellisland and legalized his marriage to Jean Armour.

Farmer once more, as he moved to Dumfriesshire, Burns must have felt wistful about what might have been. What were his feelings as he 'backward cast his e'e'?

Last days in Dumfriesshire

When Burns settled at Ellisland in 1788 with Jean Armour and the beginnings of their family, little did he know he had only eight years of life left. Into those few years he seems to have packed a lifetime. Farmer, exciseman, husband, father and collector of Scottish song, he still found time for friends and the geniality of the Dumfriesshire inns. It has been said that in this later half of his life, his talent was whittled away writing, altering and collecting Scottish songs, but that ignores his huge contribution to Scotland's cultural history. It also ignores some of his finest works such as 'Tam o' Shanter', 'Ae Fond Kiss', 'Scots Wha Hae', 'Coming Through the Rye', 'A Man's a Man for a' That', 'The Deil's awa wi' th' Exciseman' and the beautiful 'John Anderson, my Jo'.

John Anderson, My Jo

John Anderson, my jo, John,	*love, darling*
When we were first acquent,	
Your locks were like the raven,	
Your bonie brow was brent;	*unwrinkled*
But now your brow is beld, John,	*bald*
Your locks are like the snaw;	
But blessings on your frosty pow,	*white head*
John Anderson, my jo.	
John Anderson, my jo, John,	
We clamb the hill thegither;	*climbed*
And mony a canty day, John,	*happy*
We've had wi' ane anither;	
Now we maun totter down, John:	
And hand in hand we'll go,	
And sleep thegither at the foot,	
John Anderson, my Jo.	

While he was not the same man who had produced the great poems of the Mossgiel days, Burns was still master of his art. His pen was no less sharp, no less deep, if a little sadder and perhaps wiser.

> Life is but a Day at most;
> Sprung from Night – in Darkness lost:
> Hope not Sunshine every hour,
> Fear not Clouds will ever lour.
> Happiness is but a name,
> Make Content and Ease thy aim.
> Ambition is a meteor-gleam;
> Fame, a restless idel dream;
> (*Written in Friars' Carse Hermitage: first version*)

He never lost his vigour for life, or his insight, nor was his love of nature or his fellow man any less acute. And his tributes to the 'lasses' continued. At this point you could quote from 'Ae Fond Kiss' or 'O Whistle and I'll come to you, my Lad'. Remember 'Ae Fond Kiss' was written in 1791 as a final farewell to 'Clarinda', and the yearning in it signifies not only the pain of a lost love but is also an elegy to his lost hope.

Ae Fond Kiss

> Ae fond kiss, and then we sever; *One*
> Ae fareweel, and then for ever!
> Deep in heart-wrung tears I'll pledge thee,
> Warring sighs and groans I'll wage thee.
>
> Who shall say that Fortune grieves him
> While the star of hope she leaves him?
> Me, nae cheerful twinkle lights me:
> Dark despair around benights me.
>
> I'll ne'er blame my partial fancy,
> Naething could resist my Nancy:
> But to see her was to love her;
> Love but her, and love for ever.
>
> Had we never lov'd sae kindly!
> Had we never lov'd sae blindly!
> Never met – or never parted,
> We had ne'er been broken-hearted.

43

Fare-thee-weel, thou first and fairest!
Fare-thee-weel, thou best and dearest!
Thine be ilka joy and treasure,   *every*
Peace, Enjoyment, Love and Pleasure!

Ae fond kiss, and then we sever!
Ae fareweel, Alas, for ever!
Deep in heart-wrung tears I'll pledge thee,
Warring sighs and groans I'll wage thee.

At the end Burns must have looked back on his Dumfriesshire days will some fondness and contentment. Although his dreams of making a living by his art were long gone and the physical demands of his work had taken their toll on his health, Burns knew there were compensations in his wife and children and the support of true friends. Although often struck down by melancholic moods, he could always find humour in life's little ironies and incongruities. In the midst of problems and pain they lifted his spirits and allowed him to laugh at the ridiculousness of life. That is the common ground between Burns and those who share his beliefs.

SUMMING UP: Burns's contribution

When we consider his chronic health problems and his difficult, often treacherous working conditions, we can only wonder at his contribution to Scottish literature and life. We cannot emulate his greatness, but we can take heart from his courage, find compassion for our fellow man and hope for the future. Burns's work advocates living life to the full, being kind to one's neighbour, enjoying the simple pleasures and feeling grateful for the privilege. His maxim from 'Epistle to Davie' best describes the man and his philosophy:

The heart ay's the part ay   *always*
That makes us right or wrang.

The speech should finish with the toast:

> 'Ladies and Gentlemen I give you "The Immortal
> Memory of Robert Burns".'

Burns's wit

INTRODUCTION: Burns's wit – forte or foible?

Burns's wit flowed through all his writing and conversation. It
was at times corrective, at others gentle and teasing and when
directed at himself, as poet and rhymer, it was pure tongue-in-
cheek humour. Burns's wit stemmed from his instinctive love of
life and all its idiosyncracies. Pretension, hypocrisy and greed
often caused his hackles to rise and many felt the force of his
passion and anger.

From his early days of debate at the Tarbolton Bachelors'
Club, through the heady days in Edinburgh society, to the final
sallies at Dumfries, Burns never lost his passion for the lightning
thrust in conversation or the stinging barb in verse. That would
have been to deny his instincts. Maria Riddell, who suffered
more than most from the blows of his sharp pen, revealed in her
splendid obituary to Burns that she believed that poetry was not
actually his forte, but that the cut and thrust of social encounter
was where he reigned supreme:

> Many others, perhaps, may have ascended to prouder
> heights in the region of Parnassus, but none certainly ever
> outshone Burns in the charms, the sorcery, I would almost
> call it, of fascinating conversation, the spontaneous
> eloquence of social argument, or the unstudied poignancy
> of brilliant repartee.

> The rapid lightnings of his eye were always the harbingers
> of some flash of genius, whether they darted the fiery
> glances of insulted and indignant superiority, or beamed
> with the impassioned sentiment of fervent and impetuous
> affections.

The keenness of his satire was, I am almost at a loss whether to say, his forte or his foible, for though nature had endowed him with a portion of the most pointed excellence in that dangerous talent, he suffered it too often to be the vehicle of personal, and sometimes unfounded, animosities.

He paid for his mischievious wit as dearly as anyone could do. 'Twas no extravagant arithmetic', to say of him, as was said of Yorick, 'that for every ten jokes he got a hundred enemies'.

(From Maria Riddell's obituary, *Dumfries Advertiser*, 31 July 1796)

This testimony to his talents could be summed up in one line from his poem 'Epistle from Esopus to Maria' – 'A wit in folly and a fool in wit'.

Certainly Burns's reputation for delivering the sharp rebuke went before him and there were always those ill at ease in his company. But equally his charm was just as devastating and he often left the same company bedazzled by it.

So, was satire Burns's forte or foible? You could begin by looking at Burns's extremes of wit in verse with two examples from his Dumfriesshire days. The first is a spiteful note he pinned to Maria Riddell's carriage (see also 'Monody' on a lady famed for her caprice) after the row which broke up their friendship for a time:

If you rattle along like your mistress's tongue,
Your speed will out-rival the dart;
But, a fly for your load, you'll break down on the road,
If your stuff be as rotten's her heart.
(*Extempore, pinned to a lady's coach*)

and the second, a light, amusing epitaph he suggested for a friend's tombstone:

Beneath this turn lies W . . . G . . .
Nature thy loss bemoan;
When thou wouldst make a fool again –
Thy choicest model's gone.
(From Gordon Irving, *The Wit of Robert Burns*)

Burns's sojourn in Edinburgh produced many exclamations about his eloquence, wit and vigour in conversation and his pen was no less active either, whether in taking some presumptuous host or hostess down a peg or two or simply praising a fair lady. His description of Miss Burnet, Lord Monboddo's daughter, for example, in a letter to a friend, was typical of the extreme flights to which he was prone when confronted with great beauty:

> There has not been anything nearly like her in all the combinations of Beauty, Grace and Goodness, the great Creator has formed since Milton's Eve on the first day of her existence.
> (Letter to William Chambers, Edinburgh, 27 December 1786)

But the same pen wrote, in very different terms, to an eminent peeress in Edinburgh who, though never having met the poet, was desperate to have him exhibited at one of her soirées. Remembering that at the time an animal called 'The Learned Pig' was being displayed for the crowd's amusement in the Grassmarket, he replied wickedly to her invitation:

> Mr Burns will do himself the honour of waiting on Her Ladyship provided she will invite also 'The Learned Pig'.
> (From Gordon Irving, *The Wit of Robert Burns*)

Maria Riddell's question of his wit being forte or foible could be applied to any area of Burns's writing. The following on the Church, women and himself are only suggestions.

DEVELOPMENT: The Church

The poet's dislike of hypocrisy and the unrealistic strictures of the religion of the day often brought him into conflict with the Church, the clergy and pillars of the community. Verses from any of his three great satires against the Church, 'Holy Willie's Prayer', 'Address to the Unco Guid', or 'The Holy Fair', could be used. In the following verses Burns delivers a salutory slap on the wrist to the parishioners of Mauchline for their conceit and unchristian attitudes:

Ye high, exalted, virtuous Dames,
Ty'd up in godly laces,
Before ye gie poor *Frailty* names,
Suppose a change o' cases;
A dear–lov'd lad, convenience snug,
A treacherous inclination –
But, let me whisper i' your lug,   *ear*
Ye're aiblins nae temptation.   *perhaps*

Then gently scan your brother Man,
Still gentler sister Woman;
Tho' they may gang a kennin wrang,
To step aside is human:
One point must still be greatly dark,
The moving *Why* they do it;
And just as lamely can ye mark,
How far perhaps they rue it.
(*Address to the Unco Guid, or the Rigidly Righteous*)

You could also include this lighter nudge at the clergy, as Burns devilishly suggests what lies behind their sanctimonious façade:

The minister kiss't the fiddler's wife
He could na preach for thinkin o't.
(*My Love she's but a Lassie Yet*)

What should be emphasized, if speaking on this aspect of his work, is that Burns, underneath all his denunciations of the Church, was a devout believer in God and the concept of Christianity. What he railled against, apart from the false piety it engendered (beautifully illustrated in 'Holy Willie's Prayer'), was the manipulation, by fear, of an ignorant and superstitious populous. Too practical and intelligent to be indoctrinated into passivity, he often appeared to many as an athiest and a reactionary.

The lasses

If looking at the 'lasses', consult the speaker delivering 'The Toast to the Lasses' in case your material overlaps.

Burns's love of the 'lasses' is well documented, both in his life and work. They were the inspiration for his best romantic verse and they played a vital part in his existence. The following are just a few of his comments to and about women. Finding himself sitting next to pretty Miss Ainslie in church and listening to the minister loudly condemn 'obstinate sinners', Burns quickly dashed off this compliment and handed it to her:

> Fair maid, you need not take the hint,
> Nor idle texts pursue;
> 'Twas guilty sinners that he meant –
> Not angels such as you.
> (*To Miss Ainslie, while looking for a text in church*)

Other references abound:

> Their tricks an' craft hae put me daft,
> They've ta'en me in, an' a' that;
> But clear your decks, an' here's the Sex!
> I like the jads for a' that.   jades
> (*The Jolly Beggars*)

> There's ae wee faut they whiles lay to me,
> I like the lasses – Gude forgie me!
> For mony a plack they wheedle frae me   coin
> At dance or fair;
> Maybe some other thing they gie me,
> They weel can spare.
> (*Epistle to J. Lapraik*)

His wit about women is very different from that about the Church. There is nothing he would change about the 'lasses'. He, unlike many men, then and now, doesn't feel threatened by them. They and all their intricacies are a constant source of delight. To finish this theme and lead into the next you could recite 'Advice to the Mauchline Belles'. In this poem Burns casts himself in the role of the fox in the farmyard.

O leave novels, ye Mauchline belles,
Ye're safer at your spinning-wheel;
Such witching books are baited hooks
For rakish rooks like Rob Mossgiel;
Your fine Tom Jones and Grandisons,
They make your youthful fancies reel;
They heat your brains, and fire your veins,
And then you're prey for Rob Mossgiel.

Beware a tongue that's smoothly hung,
A heart that warmly seems to feel;
That feeling heart but acts a part –
'Tis rakish art in Rob Mossgiel.
The frank address, the soft caress,
Are worse than poisoned darts of steel;
The frank address, and politesse,
Are all finesse in Rob Mossgiel.

Burns on himself

Burns's wit about himself takes many forms. There are the marvellously relaxed, seemingly casually construed lines in 'Extempore Epistle to Gavin Hamilton, Esq.' (stanzas on 'naething'):

The Poet may jingle and rhyme
In hopes of a laureate wreathing,
And when he has wasted his time
He's kindly rewarded with naething.

And now, I must mount on the wave,
My voyage perhaps there is death in:
What is a watery grave?
The drowning a Poet is naething.

In another poem, 'Epistle to J. Lapraik', a smiling assurance is evident:

I am nae poet, in a sense,
But just a rhymer like by chance;
An' hae to learning nae pretence;
Yet, what the matter?
Whene'er my muse does on me glance,
I jingle at her.

> Your critic-folk may cock their nose,
> And say, 'How can you e'er propose,
> You wha ken hardly verse frae prose,
> To mak a sang?'
> But, by your leaves, my learned foes,
> Ye're maybe wrang.
>
> Gie me ae spark o' nature's fire,
> That's a' the learning I desire;
> Then tho' I drudge thro' dub an' mire   *puddles*
> At pleugh or cart,
> My muse, tho' hamely in attire,
> May touch the heart.

In all these verses Burns's light touch shows his complete mastery of wry humour. His mockery of the poet's life and all its contrariness also reveals that had he the choice, he would change 'naething'. The last verse from 'Epistle to a Young Friend' is magnanimous Burns at his best:

> Adieu, dear, amiable Youth!
> Your heart can ne'er be wanting!
> May Prudence, Fortitude, and Truth,
> Erect your brow undaunting!
> In ploughman phrase, 'God send you speed'
> Still daily to grow wiser;
> And may ye better reck the rede,   *attend to the advice*
> Than ever did th' Adviser.

SUMMING UP: wit and wisdom

In summing up Burns's wit, whether you decide it was forte or foible, you could suggest that the core of it comes from his roots in the soil of Ayrshire. As a farmer, Burns's constant companions were death, disease and destruction or alternately the abundance of a plentiful harvest, the beauty of a summer day or the sensuous charms of a pretty woman. These extremities polarized his thought. He had little time for the affectation or unkindness born out of idle minds. He loved beauty: the physical and the spiritual, and in hypocrisy, greed and conceit he found only ugliness. He used his wit as a whiplash against anything and anyone he found wanting in the warmth of human compassion, but equally he applauded life's fleeting joys, held up to the light its extremities of behaviour and hoped that someday:

> That Man to Man, the world o'er,
> Shall brothers be for a' that!
> (*A Man's a Man for a' That*)

You should finish the speech with thoughts of what we can learn today from Burns's work and wisdom, remembering that wit was only one arrow in his quiver.

The speech should finish with the toast:

> 'Ladies and Gentlemen I give you "The Immortal Memory of Robert Burns".'

Ploughman poet or intellectual?

Edinburgh dubbed Burns the 'ploughman poet' during his first visit to the city, after the publication of the Kilmarnock edition of his work in 1786. Initially mistaken for some inspired rustic, a notion he enjoyed perpetrating, it quickly became obvious that, although an Ayrshire farmer, he was wisely schooled and widely read, possessed of a fine mind, an observant eye and a lively tongue. At any gathering his companions could find themselves either damned or charmed, depending on his level of sufferance.

INTRODUCTION: the different sides of Burns's talent

You could begin this theme with Lord Byron's description of Burns's diversities of mind, after reading the unpublished letters.

They are full of oaths and obscene songs. What an antithetical mind! – tenderness, toughness – delicacy, courseness – sentiment, sensuality – soaring and grovelling, dirt and deity – all mixed up in that one compound of inspired clay!

In many ways that 'compound of inspired clay' typifies the Scottish character and its extremes of existence, the combination of practicality and emotion. One reason for Burns's immediate success was that the majority of the population recognized in themselves and their lives, all that Burns had dared to record on paper.

But Burns's literary insights did not just tumble from his pen. They were the result of a great deal of thought and effort. His early masterpieces were composed in the fields during the day and in the evening harnessed, refined and honed to perfection. 'Ploughman poet' perhaps, but his work was also a potent combination of innate surety, a solid education, a childhood imagination stimulated by old Scots songs and tales, and hours of polishing and reassessing his thoughts. Behind the seeming naivety and deceptive simplicity of his best-known work lies the hand of a master craftsman.

To illustrate this contrast you could quote verses from 'The Rigs o' Barley' and 'Death and Dr Hornbook', both from the Ayrshire years. Each show a different side of his talent:

> It was upon a Lammas night,
> When corn rigs are bonie,
> Beneath the moon's unclouded light,
> I held awa to Annie;
> The time flew by, wi' tentless heed,
> Till 'tween the late and early,
> Wi' sma' persuasion she agreed
> To see me thro' the barley.
>
> The sky was blue, the wind was still,
> The moon was shining clearly;
> I set her down, wi' right good will,
> Amang the rigs o' barley:
> I ken't her heart was a' my ain;
> I lov'd her most sincerely;
> I kiss'd her owre and owre again,
> Amang the rigs o' barley.
> (*The Rigs o' Barley*)

Burns describes the heady pleasures of a warm summer's evening, but equally, with consummate skill, in 'Death and Dr Hornbook', he sets the scene, albeit tongue-in-cheek, for a supernatural tale:

> But this that I am gaun to tell,   *going*
> Which lately on a night befel,
> Is just as true's the Deil's in hell
> Or Dublin city:
> That e'er he nearer comes oursel
> 'S a muckle pity.
>
> The clachan yill had made me   *village ale –*
>   canty,   *merry*
> I was na fou, but just had plenty;   *drunk*
> I stacher'd whyles, but yet took   *staggered at times –*
>   tent ay   *care*
> To free the ditches;
> An' hillocks, stanes, an' bushes, kenn'd ay
> Frae ghaists an' witches.
>
> The rising moon began to glowre   *stare*
> The distant Cumnock hill out-owre:
> To count her horns, wi' a' my pow'r,
> I set mysel;
> But whether she had three or four,
> I cou'd na tell.

DEVELOPMENT: *ploughman poet or intellectual*

You could say that Burns was 'ploughman poet' in that he found his inspiration in the countryside and the people he came into contact with in the daily round of rural life. But, just as importantly, this was the background in which his character was formed: the disciplines he endured, both behind the plough and as he worked late into the night with his pen, saw Burns through his most difficult days.

It was that character, combined with a commanding presence and great personal charm, which earned him as many laurels in Edinburgh as his poetry had done.

In great demand, he enjoyed airing his sharp wit and intellect, impressing the university's professors, overpowering the city burghers and being the 'darling' of society. By the time Burns left Edinburgh for Dumfriesshire, the powers of his intellect could hardly be in doubt. But 'ploughman poet' he was and so he would stay. We look back now and wonder why, after so much critical acclaim and adulation, nothing was done to help Burns live by his writing, why indeed Scotland so rarely rewards its own. Perhaps his wit was just too sharp.

Edinburgh, fortunately, had little effect on his work: for he refused advice, often given, to write in English and continued instead to communicate in the language of the people. His later works in Dumfriesshire show that he had not lost his touch in his ability to appeal directly to the heart or mind.

You could recite verses from the stirring 'Scots Wha Hae' ('Bruce to his men at Bannockburn'):

> Scots, wha hae wi' Wallace bled,   *who have*
> Scots, wham Bruce has aften led,   *whom*
> Welcome to your gory bed,
> Or to victorie!
>
> By oppressions's woes and pains!
> By your sons in servile chains!
> We will drain our dearest veins,
> But they shall be free!
>
> Lay the proud usurpers low!
> Tyrants fall in ev'ry foe!
> Liberty's in ev'ry blow! –
> Let us do or die!

Or the rousing 'The Deil's awa wi' th' Exciseman':

> The Deil's awa, the deil's awa,
> The Deil's awa wi' th' Exciseman,
> He's danc'd awa, he's danc'd awa,
> He's danc'd awa wi' th' Exciseman.

We'll mak our maut and we'll brew our drink,
We'll laugh, sing and rejoice, man!
And mony braw thanks to the meikle   *hearty – big*
    black Deil
That danc'd awa wi' th' Exciseman.

There's threesome reels, there's foursome reels,
There's hornpipes and strathspeys, man,
But the ae best dance e'er cam to the Land,
Was 'The Deil's awa wi' th' Exciseman'.

SUMMING UP: Burns – a unique poet

By the end of this speech it should be apparent that the 'plough-man poet' cannot be separated from the intellectual. You should point out that Burns has a unique place in Scotland's literary history, in keeping alive the traditional Scots language used by his predecessors Allan Ramsay and Robert Fergusson. Burns's education in rural Ayrshire, made possible by his father's fervent belief in learning (and he was not alone in this), ensured that he was not only on a par with those he met in the capital but in most cases superior.

Burns was a ploughman poet, to all intents and purposes, not in the patronizing terms of the Edinburgh burghers, but in the sense that his work affected his whole being and strengthened his passions and beliefs. But he was also an intellectual in his ability to translate life's pain and passions into something beautiful and enduring and to try to make some order, however strained, out of man's existence. That is why we gather to celebrate his life. 'Ploughman poet' or intellectual, it does not really matter. It is the man and his courage in a hard fought fight that we salute.

The speech should finish with the toast:

> 'Ladies and Gentlemen I give you "The Immortal Memory of Robert Burns".'

The Other Speeches

Appreciation of 'The Immortal Memory'

After 'The Immortal Memory' is delivered, the piper plays a tune, and then a short 'Appreciation' of the speech is usually given, either by a guest or the Chairman himself. It has the dual role of being a thank you to the speaker for his skill and insight and a further opportunity to reflect on Burns's life and work and how it can inspire us today. 'The Appreciation' should last no longer than five minutes and should really be given by someone with a wide knowledge of Burns.

'The Appreciation' is followed by the two other compulsory speeches, 'The Toast to the Lasses' and 'The Reply'. These should last no longer than ten minutes and should change the mood of the evening from serious thought to amusement and hilarity.

'The toast to the Lasses'

As explained earlier, this toast was originally a thank you to the ladies for preparing the food for the evening and a time to toast the 'lasses' in Burns's life. Today's audience will expect to hear a witty speech about the female sex, with a few nudges and sly digs about their idiosyncracies and foibles. It should, however, *never* be offensive and should definitely end on a conciliatory note. The speech should blend modern observations with quotations and sentiments from Burns's work. You should use examples from Burns's work, showing that the 'lasses' were just as difficult to understand in his day. Kate, Tam o' Shanter's wife, deserves a mention as perhaps does Willie Wastle's wife. Clarinda and Maria Riddell drove Burns to heights of frenzy and frustration. In 'Monody' (on a lady famed for her caprice) the full force of Burns's satire is unleashed on Maria Riddell, but in 'The Last

Time I Came o'er the Moor' he describes his despair and exasperation with this woman, and how she has affected him. Emotions not unknown in both sexes.

The Last Time I Came O'er the Moor

The last time I came o'er the moor,
And left Maria's dwelling,
What throes, what tortures passing cure,
Were in my bosom swelling:
Condemned to see my rival's reign,
While I in secret languish;
To feel a fire in every vein,
Yet dare not speak my anguish.

Love's veriest wretch, despairing, I
Fain, fain my crime would cover:
The unweeting groan, the bursting sigh,   *unwitting*
Betray the guilty lover.
I know my doom must be despair:
Thou wilt nor canst relieve me;
But, O Maria, hear my prayer,
For pity's sake, forgive me!

The music of thy tongue I heard,
Nor wist while it enslaved me;
I saw thine eyes, yet nothing feared,
Till fears no more had saved me.
The unwary sailor thus, aghast,
The wheeling torrent viewing,
Mid circling horrors yields at last
In overwhelming ruin!

Frustrated, thwarted, or simply baffled, Burns adored the 'lasses' and you should finish this speech with a tribute to them before asking the men to rise and drink: 'The Toast to the Lasses'.

'The Reply'

'The Reply' from the 'lasses' should also be a humorous speech, in turn detailing men's vices and lack of virtue. You could quote from 'Tam o' Shanter':

And at his elbow, Souter Johnny,	*Cobbler*
His ancient, trusty, drouthy, crony;	*thirsty*
Tam lo'ed him like a very brither;	
They had been fou for weeks thegither.	
The night drave on wi' sangs and clatter;	
And ay the ale was growing better:	
The Landlady and Tam grew gracious	
Wi' favours secret, sweet and precious:	

You could also quote from 'Willie brew'd a Peck o' Maut' where Burns beautifully describes the idiocy produced by alcohol, as the three cronies insist they are not drunk:

We are na fou, we're nae that fou,	*drunk*
But just a drappie in our e'e;	*drop – eye*
The cock may craw, the day may daw,	*dawn*
And ay we'll taste the barley bree.	*brew, juice*

Here are we met, three merry boys,
Three merry boys, I trow, are we;
And mony a night we've merry been,
And mony mae we hope to be!   *more*

Again, like the previous speech, after pointing out the imperfections of the opposite sex, it should end on a conciliatory note, but leaving no doubt as to where Burns's allegiance lay.

When ance life's day draws near the	*once –*
gloamin,	*twilight*
Then fareweel vacant, careless roamin;	
An' fareweel cheerfu' tankards foamin,	
An' social noise:	
An' fareweel dear, deluding woman,	
The joy of joys!	
(*Epistle to James Smith*)	

Other toasts

At many suppers there is a toast to the town or city and a toast to
'Scotland' or 'Scotia' is popular. At dinners abroad it is common
to toast Scotland, but also the adopted country. Other frequent
toasts within the Burns Club Federation are the Federation itself or
'Kindred clubs'. If you have a Federation representative at your
supper, invite him or her to reply and ask them to explain about
the organization and its aims.

Poems and Songs

Once the speeches are over the evening continues with songs and recitations from Burns's work. They should contrast with one another to create different moods from the gentle intimacy of 'To a Mouse' to the rollicking fun of 'The Deil's awa wi' th' Exciseman'. Standard favourites for recitations are 'Tam o' Shanter', 'Holy Willie's Prayer', 'Address to the Unco Guid, or the Rigidly Righteous' and 'To a Mouse', but others such as 'The Auld Farmer's New-Year Morning Salutation to his Auld Mare, Maggie', 'Death and Dr Hornbook', 'Extempore Epistle to Gavin Hamilton' and 'The Twa Dogs' are equally enjoyed.

Any of Burns's songs can be sung. The singers will have suggestions and know which they perform best. 'A Red, Red Rose', 'The Banks o' Doon', 'Willie brew'd a Peck o' Maut', 'Ca' the Yowes to the Knowes', 'O Whistle, and I'll come to you, my Lad' and 'A Highland Lad my love was Born' from 'The Jolly Beggars' are all popular choices. Each singer sings two or three songs and there is usually one duet.

In the following pages you will find some of these poems and songs with notes on their origins. Whichever you choose for your evening's entertainment, you could, by way of an introduction, give a brief history of each poem and song before it is performed.

Tam o' Shanter

A favourite at every dinner, Burns's tall tale is a splendid piece of entertainment and a fine example of his fertile imagination. Written in a day (late in 1790) as he walked up and down the bank of the River Nith, behind Ellisland, his fervour of mental activity seems captured in the pace of the poem. Listening to it delivered by a good speaker you will find yourself carried along by the speed of the action and consequently exhausted at the finish. Rousing, amusing and with the gently wagging finger at the end, it is a complete work of art in every sense.

No doubt Burns found inspiration in many places for the action, the characters and the setting, but we know that it came about at the instigation of Francis Grose when he was looking for a supernatural tale for inclusion in the second volume of his *Antiquities of Scotland*, published in 1791. In exchange for Grose's promise to include a drawing of Alloway Kirkyard, where his father was buried, Burns produced his ripping yarn to accompany the illustration.

According to Jean Armour, Burns had great fun producing the work, she could hear him laughing and howling with delight all day long. The source of his inspiration came from earlier days in Ayrshire. Alloway's supposedly haunted kirkyard provided an eerie backdrop for Tam's meeting with the other world and the characters of Tam and his crony Souter Johnny were based on two individuals whom Burns remembered from his Kirkoswald days.

Shanter was the name of a farm steading between Turnberry and Culzean and the farmer Douglas Graham was the model for Tam. Given to drinking late in the pubs in Ayr after the markets closed, Graham and his friend John Davidson (Souter Johnny) often rolled home the worse for wear. Graham's wife complained about these constant binges, warning they would end in disaster one day.

Alloway Kirkyard

Thus Graham provided Burns with the theme of the poem and the setting of Alloway's haunted kirkyard. After one of his market-day trips he lost his bonnet with the day's takings inside. Trembling at the thought of explaining to his wife, he made up a tale (plausible he believed, in his drunken stupor) about being set upon by witches in the churchyard. 'Cutty Sark' was also based on a Kirkoswald woman, Kate Stein, a fortune teller reputed to be a witch.

Tam o' Shanter
A Tale

'Of Brownyis and of Bogillis full is this Buke.'
Gawin Douglas

When chapman billies leave the street,	*packman fellows*
And drouthy neebors neebors meet;	*thirsty*
As market days are wearing late,	
An' folk begin to tak the gate;	*road*
While we sit bousing at the nappy,	*ale*
An' gettin fou and unco happy,	*drunk – very*
We think na on the lang Scots miles,	
The mosses, waters, slaps, and stiles,	*bogs – gaps*
That lie between us and our hame,	
Whare sits our sulky sullen dame,	
Gathering her brows like gathering storm,	
Nursing her wrath to keep it warm.	

This truth fand honest Tam o' Shanter, *found*
As he frae Ayr ae night did canter:
(Auld Ayr, wham ne'er a town surpasses
For honest men and bonny lasses).

O Tam! hadst thou but been sae wise
As taen thy ain wife Kate's advice!
She tauld thee weel thou was a skellum, *rogue*
A blethering, blustering drunken blellum;
That frae November till October
Ae market-day thou was na sober;

That ilka melder wi' the miller   *every*
Thou sat as lang as thou had siller;   *money*
That every naig was ca'd a shoe on   *shod*
The smith and thee gat roaring fou on;
That at the L–d's house, ev'n on Sunday,
Thou drank wi' Kirkton Jean till Monday.
She prophesy'd that, late or soon,
Thou wad be found deep drown'd in Doon;
Or catch'd wi' warlocks in the   *wizards –*
    mirk   *darkness*
By Alloway's auld haunted kirk.

Ah, gentle dames! it gars me greet   *makes – weep*
To think how mony counsels sweet,
How mony lengthen'd, sage advices
The husband from the wife despises!

But to our tale: – Ae market night,
Tam had got planted unco right;
Fast by an ingle, bleezing finely,   *fire*
Wi' reaming swats, that drank   *foaming – new ale*
    divinely;
And at his elbow, Souter Johnny,   *Cobbler*
His ancient, trusty, drouthy crony,   *thirsty*
Tam lo'ed him like a very brither;
They had been fou for weeks thegither.
The night drave on wi' sangs and clatter;
And ay the ale was growing better:
The Landlady and Tam grew gracious
Wi' favours secret, sweet and precious:
The Souter tauld his queerest stories;
The landlord's laugh was ready chorus:
The storm without might rair and rustle,   *roar*
Tam did na mind the storm a whistle.

Care, mad to see a man sae happy,
E'en drown'd himself amang the nappy;
As bees flee hame wi' lades o' treasure,   *loads*
The minutes wing'd their way wi' pleasure:
Kings may be blest, but Tam was glorious,
O'er a' the ills o' life victorious!

But pleasures are like poppies spread,
You seize the flowr, its bloom is shed;
Or like the snow falls in the river,
A moment white – then melts for ever;
Or like the borealis race
That flit ere you can point their place,
Or like the rainbows lovely form
Evanishing amid the storm.
Nae man can tether time or tide;
The hour approaches Tam maun ride;   *must*
That hour o' night's black arch the key-stane,
That dreary hour he mounts his beast in;
And sic a night he taks the road in
As ne'er poor sinner was abroad in.

The wind blew as 'twad blawn its last; *would have*
The rattling show'rs rose on the blast;
The speedy gleams the darkness swallow'd;
Loud, deep, and lang, the thunder bellow'd:
That night a child might understand
The Deil had business on his hand.

Weel mounted on his gray mare, Meg,
A better never lifted leg,
Tam skelpit on thro' dub and mire, *rattled – puddle*
Despising wind, and rain, and fire;
Whiles holding fast his gude blue bonnet;
Whiles crooning o'er some auld Scots *humming*
 sonnet;
Whiles glow'ring round wi' prudent cares *gazing*
Lest bogles catch him unawares: *hobgoblins*
Kirk-Alloway was drawing nigh,
Whare ghaists and houlets nightly cry. *owls*

By this time he was' cross the ford,
Whare in the snaw the chapman smoor'd; *smothered*
And past the birks and meikle stane *birches – big*
Whare drunken Charlie brak's neck-bane;
And thro' the whins, and by the   *gorse –*
 cairn   *pile of stones*
Whare hunters fand the murder'd bairn; *child*

And near the thorn, aboon the well,   *above*
Whare Mungo's mither hang'd hersel.
Before him Doon pours all his floods,
The doubling storm roars thro' the woods;
The lightnings flash frae pole to pole;
Near and more near the thunders roll:
When, glimmering thro' the groaning trees,
Kirk-Alloway seem'd in a bleeze;
Thro' ilka bore the beams were   *every cranny*
   glancing;
And loud resounded mirth and dancing.

Inspiring bold John Barleycorn!
What dangers thou canst make us scorn!
Wi' tippenny we fear nae evil;
Wi' usquabae we'll face the devil!   *whisky*
The swats sae ream'd in Tammie's noddle,
Fair play, he car'd na deils a boddle.
But Maggie stood right sair astonish'd,
Till, by the heel and hand admonish'd,
She ventur'd forward on the light;
And, vow! Tam saw an unco sight   *in sooth! – marvellous*

Warlocks and witches in a dance;
Nae cotillion brent new frae France,   *brand-new*
But hornpipes, jigs, strathspeys and reels,
Put life and mettle in their heels.
A winnock-bunker in the east,   *window-recess*
There sat auld Nick, in shape o' beast;
A towzie tyke, black, grim and large,   *shaggy dog*
To gie them music was his charge:
He screw'd the pipes and gart them   *made –*
   skirl   *scream*
Till roof and rafters a' did dirl.   *vibrate*
Coffins stood round, like open presses,   *cupboards*
That shaw'd the dead in their last dresses;
And, by some devilish cantraip sleight,   *weird trick*
Each in its cauld hand held a light –
By which heroic Tam was able
To note upon the haly table

A murderer's banes, in gibbet-airns;   *irons*
Twa span-lang, wee, unchristen'd bairns;
A thief new-cutted frae a rape,   *from a rope*
Wi' his last gasp his gab did gape;   *mouth*
Five tomahawks wi' blude red-rusted;
Five scymitars wi' murder crusted;
A garter which a babe had strangled;
A knife a father's throat had mangled –
Whom his ain son o' life bereft –
The grey hairs yet stack to the   *stuck to the*
   heft;   *handle*
Wi' mair of horrible and awefu',
Which ev'n to name wad be unlawfu'.

As Tammie glowr'd, amaz'd and curious,   *stared*
The mirth and fun grew fast and furious:
The piper loud and louder blew,
The dancers quick and quicker flew:
They reel'd, they set, they cross'd, they
   cleekit,   *took hands*
Till ilka carlin swat and reekit,   *witch – steamed*
And coost her duddies to the wark,   *threw off – clothes*
And linket at it in her sark!   *set to it – shift*

Now Tam, O Tam! had thae been   *these –*
   queans,   *young women*
A' plump and strapping in their teens!
Their sarks, instead o' creeshie flannen,   *greasy nannel*
Been snaw-white seventeen hunder linnen! –
Thir breeks o' mine, my only pair,   *These*
That ance were plush, o' gude blue hair,
I wad hae gi'en them off my hurdies   *buttocks*
For ae blink o' the bonie burdies!   *birds*

But wither'd beldams, auld and droll,
Rigwoodie hags wad spean a foal,
Lowping and flinging on a   *Leaping –*
   crummock,   *stick wiih a crooked head*
I wonder didna turn thy stomach.

But Tam kend what was what fu'
brawlie: *quite well*
There was ae winsome wench and wawlie,   *comely*
That night enlisted in the core   *corps*
(Lang after kend on Carrick shore:
For mony a beast to dead she shot,   *death*
And perish'd mony a bonny boat,
And shook baith meikle corn and bear,   *much barley*
And held the country-side in fear).
Her cutty sark, o' Paisley   *short shift –*
harn,   *coarse linen*
That while a lassie she had worn,
In longitude tho' sorely scanty,
It was her best, and she was vauntie.   *proud of it*
Ah! little kend thy reverend grannie,
That sark she coft for her wee Nannie,   *bought*
Wi' two pund Scots ('twas a' her   *3s. 6d. English*
riches),
Wad ever grac'd a dance of witches!

But here my Muse her wing maun cour   *fold*
Sic flights are far beyond her pow'r;
To sing how Nannie lap and flang   *leaped – kicked*
(A souple jade she was and strang),
And how Tam stood like ane bewitch'd
And thought his very een enrich'd;
Even Satan glowr'd, and   *gazed and*
fidg'd fu' fain,   *hitched his shoulders in glee*
And hotch'd and blew wi' might and   *squirmed*
main,
Till first ae caper, syne anither,   *then*
Tam tint his reason a' thegither   *lost – altogether*
And roars out 'Weel done, Cutty-sark!'
And in an instant all was dark;
And scarcely had he Maggie rallied,
When out the hellish legion sallied.

As bees bizz out wi' angry fyke,   *fret*
When plundering herds assail their byke; *herd-boys — nest*
As open pussie's mortal foes,   *the hare's*
When, pop! she starts before their nose;
As eager runs the market-crowd,
When 'Catch the thief!' resounds aloud;
So Maggie runs — the witches follow,
Wi' mony an eldritch skreech and hollow. *frightful*

Ah, Tam! Ah, Tam! thou' ll get thy fairin! *reward, treat*
In hell they'll roast thee like a herrin!
In vain thy Kate awaits thy comin!
Kate soon will be a woefu' woman!
Now, do thy speedy utmost, Meg,
And win the key-stane of the brig;   *reach*
There, at them thou thy tail may toss:
A running stream they dare na cross.
But ere the key-stane she could make,
The fient a tail she had to shake!   *No tail had she*
For Nannie, far before the rest,
Hard upon noble Maggie prest,
And flew at Tam wi' furious ettle: *endeavour*
But little wist she Maggie's mettle —
Ae spring brought off her master hale,   *whole*
But left behind her ain grey tail:
The carlin claught her by the rump,   *clutched*
And left poor Maggie scarce a stump.

Now, wha this tale o' truth shall read,
Ilk man and mother's son, take heed:
Whene'er to drink you are inclin'd,
Or cutty sarks run in your mind,
Think! ye may buy the joys o'er dear,
Remember Tam o' Shanter's mare.

O Whistle, and I'll come to you, my Lad

Completed in 1793 during the Dumfriesshire years, this song was written for Jean Lorimer, a local beauty, daughter of a successful farmer, whose land lay across the River Nith from Ellisland. Burns later changed the last line of the chorus to 'Thy Jeanie will venture wi' you, my lad', saying Jean had insisted on it. A regular visitor to her home, Kemmishall, Burns, undoubtedly inspired by her looks and spirited personality, described her as 'a fair dame whom the Graces have attired in witchcraft, and whom the Loves have armed with lightning'. She is 'The Lassie wi' the Lint-white Locks', the heroine of 'Craigieburn Wood' and his 'Chloris' in other songs. Sadly the fates which Burns saw as bestowing so many gifts upon her in youth, deserted her in later life.

At the age of 18, the year this song was finished, she refused an offer of marriage from one of Burns's fellow excise officers, choosing instead to run away with a young Englishman named Whelpdale. After a wedding at Gretna Green they settled on a farm at Barnhill, near Moffat, but within a few months he went bankrupt and disappeared. She returned to her parents' home and seeming security, but her father lost his fortune and began drinking, leaving her finally reduced to working in service to support herself.

Her latter years were spent in Edinburgh as a housekeeper to a family in Blacket Place. When her health began to fail and she could no longer work, her employer kindly provided her with a small flat in Nicolson Square, where she spent the rest of her days. She died in 1831 at the age of 56 and was buried in Preston Street Cemetery, Newington. Seventy years later the Edinburgh Ninety Burns Club erected a memorial granite cross over her grave with the inscription 'This stone marks the grave of Jean Lorimer, the "Chloris" and "Lassie wi' the Lint-white Locks" of the poet Burns. Born, 1775; died, 1831. Erected under the auspices of the Ninety Burns Club, Edinburgh, 1901.'

O Whistle, and I'll come to you, my Lad
Tune – O Whistle, and I'll come to you, my Lad

Chorus – O whistle, and I'll come to you, my lad,
  O whistle, and I'll come to you, my lad;
  Tho' father and mother and a' should gae mad,
  O whistle, and I'll come to you, my lad.

  But warily tent, when ye come to court me, *watch*
  And come na unless the back-yett be a-jee; *gate – ajar*
  Syne up the back-style, and let naebody see, *Then*
  And come as ye were na coming to me,
  And come as ye were na coming to me.

  At kirk or at market, whene'er ye meet me,
  Gang by me as tho' that ye car'd nae a flie; *Go – fly*
  But steal me a blink o' your bonie black e'e, *glance*
  Yet look as ye were na looking at me,
  Yet look as ye were na looking at me.

  Ay vow and protest that ye carena for me,
  And *whyles* ye may lightly my *sometimes – undervalue*
   beauty a wee; *– a little*
  But court na anither, tho' joking ye be,
  For fear that she wyle your fancy frae me, *lure*
  For fear that she wyle your fancy frae me.

Holy Willie's Prayer

Burns's glorious hypocrite 'Holy Willie' is still instantly
recognizable today. With wonderful irony, he delivers a lash
upon his own back in every line. One of Burns's finest pieces of
work, it was written in the summer of 1785 when his landlord
and friend Gavin Hamilton was finally absolved by higher
church courts of not keeping the Sabbath. The chief instigator of
the prosecution was William Fisher, a church elder and member

of the Kirk Session of Mauchline Parish Church, which first 'tried' Hamilton for such crimes as picking potatoes on Sunday and not attending church. A Mauchline man by birth, Hamilton lived there with his wife and young family, practising as a lawyer and administering the poor fund. A kind-hearted and generous friend to many, he was the very antitheses of William Fisher.

Fisher, born the son of a farmer in 1737, became an elder of Mauchline Church in 1772. A gossiping, smug, zealous upholder of strict Calvinist tenets, he came unstuck in 1790, when he was publicly rebuked by the minister William Auld for drunkenness, and although there is no church record, it is also believed that he was charged with stealing from the poor box. He froze to death in a ditch near Mauchline on 13 February 1809.

Burns initially circulated the poem amongst friends as it was considered too strident an attack on the Church to be published. It was only in 1799, three years after his death, that it was finally printed, and then only as a leaflet, by a Glasgow publisher.

Holy Willie's Prayer

And Send the Godly in a pet to pray. – Pope

O Thou that in the heavens does dwell!
Wha, as it pleases best Thysel,
Sends ane to heaven and ten to h–ll,
A' for Thy glory;
And no for ony guid or ill
They've done before Thee!

I bless and praise Thy matchless might,
When thousands Thou hast left in night,
That I am here before Thy sight,
For gifts and grace
A burning and a shining light,·
To a' this place.

What was I, or my generation,
That I should get such exaltation?
I, wha deserv'd most just damnation
For broken laws,
Sax thousand years ere my creation
Thro' Adam's cause.

When frae my mither's womb I fell,
Thou might hae plungèd me in hell,
To gnash my gums, to weep and wail,
In burnin lakes,
Where damnèd devils roar and yell,
Chain'd to their stakes.

Yet I am here, a chosen sample,
To show Thy grace is great and ample;
I'm here, a pillar o' Thy temple,
Strong as a rock;
A guide, a ruler, and example
To a' Thy flock.

O L—d, Thou kens what zeal I bear,
When drinkers drink, an' swearers swear,
An' singin' there, an' dancin' here,
Wi' great and sma';
For I am keepit by Thy fear,
Free frae them a'.

But yet, O L—d, confess I must,
At times I'm fash'd wi' fleshly lust;   *troubled*
And sometimes too in warldly trust
Vile Self gets in:
But Thou remembers we are dust,
Defil'd wi' sin.

O L—d – yestreen – Thou kens – wi Meg
Thy pardon I sincerely beg:
O, may't ne'er be a livin plague,
To my dishonor!
And I'll ne'er lift a lawless leg
Again upon her!

Besides, I further maun avow,
Wi' Leezie's lass – three times – I trow
But L–d, that Friday I was fou   *drunk*
When I cam near her;
Or else, Thou kens, Thy servant true
Wad never steer her.   *meddle with*

Maybe Thou lets this fleshly thorn
Buffet Thy servant e'en and morn
Lest he owre proud and high should turn
That he's sae gifted:
If sae, Thy hand maun e'en be borne
Until Thou lift it.

L–d bless Thy chosen in this place,
For here Thou has a chosen race;
But G–d confound their stubborn face,
And blast their name,
Wha bring their rulers to disgrace
And public shame.

L–d mind Gaun Hamilton's deserts;
He drinks, and swears, and plays at cartes,   *cards*
Yet has sae mony takin arts   *popular*
Wi' Great and Sma',
Frae G–d's ain Priest the people's hearts
He steals awa.

And when we chasten'd him therefore
Thou kens how he bred sic a splore,   *disturbance*
And set the warld in a roar
O' laughin at us:
Curse Thou his basket and his store
Kail and potatoes.

L–d hear my earnest cry and pray'r
Against that Presbytry of Ayr!
Thy strong right hand, L–d make it bare
Upo' their heads!
L–d visit them and dinna spare,
For their misdeeds!

O L–d, my G–d, that glib-tongu'd Aiken,
My very heart and flesh are quakin,
To think how I sat, sweatin, shakin,
And – wi' dread,
While Auld, wi' hingin lip gaed sneakin   *sneaky*
And hid his head.

L–d in Thy day o' vengeance try him!
L–d visit them wha did employ him!
And pass not in Thy mercy by them,
Nor hear their prayer,
But for Thy people's sake destroy them,
And dinna spare!

But L–d remember me and mine
Wi' mercies temporal and divine;
That I for grace and gear may shine,
Excell'd by nane!
And a' the glory shall be Thine,
AMEN! AMEN!

The Banks o' Doon

The story behind this song is a sad one. It is a lament for the fate
of Peggy Kennedy at the hands of her 'fause lover', Captain
Andrew McDowall of Logan. The daughter of Robert Kennedy
of Daljarroch and a niece of the poet's friend Gavin Hamilton,
Peggy first met Burns in Mauchline in 1785. Just 17 years of age
and already a beauty, she inspired Burns to write the song
'Young Peggy' as a tribute to her. At that point in her life she
was already involved with McDowall and some time later after a
'secret ceremony' arranged by him, she believed they were
married.

In 1794 she gave birth to their daughter at the same time as
McDowall inherited his father's estates. He suddenly had the
marriage declared unlawful and proceeded to marry the
daughter of a wealthy Dumfriesshire laird. An ambitious man,
McDowall was already the MP for Wigton by the age of 25, and

now a prosperous alliance with another wealthy family in the district was no more than expedient.

In a court battle in 1795 Peggy tried to have their marriage legalized and so legitimize their daughter, but she died before the court could come to a decision. Three years later the Constitutional Court of the Church formally recognized the marriage, but we can only imagine how McDowall managed to have this overruled in the Court of Session. Their daughter, however, was awarded the sum of 3000 pounds, a huge amount in those days, in solatium for her mother's ordeal.

Burns must have had a sixth sense about Peggy Kennedy. In his original letter to her, alongside the song 'Young Peggy', he had wished her good fortune and hoped 'that the snares of villainy never beset you in the road of life'. His song is an everlasting reminder of her suffering and McDowall's treachery.

The Banks o' Doon

Tune – Caledonian Hunt's Delight

Ye banks and braes o' bonie Doon,
How can ye bloom sae fresh and fair!
How can ye chant, ye little birds,
And I sae weary fu' o' care!
Thou'll break my heart, thou warbling bird
That wantons thro' the flowering thorn:
Thou minds me o' departed joys,
Departed, never to return.

Aft hae I rov'd by bonie Doon,
To see the rose and woodbine twine;
And ilka bird sang o' its luve,   *every*
And fondly sae did I o' mine;
Wi' lightsome heart I pu'd a rose,
Fu' sweet upon its thorny tree;
And my fause luver staw my rose,   *false*
But ah! he left the thorn wi' me.

The Auld Farmer's New-Year Morning Salutation to his Auld Mare Maggie

This nostalgic look at man's companionship with the animals who share his life, the momentous milestones and the daily grind, beautifully expresses the feelings of all animal lovers everywhere. Burns chose New Year and the 'ripp of corn' to signify hope and security and as the farmer reminisces about the past and the bonds that he and Maggie share, he assures her of a safe haven for the rest of her days.

Written in 1786 at Mossgiel, the poem is similar in sentiment to 'John Anderson, my Jo'.

The Auld Farmer's New-Year Morning Salutation to his Auld Mare, Maggie

On giving her the accustomed ripp of corn to hansel in the New-Year

A guid New-year I wish thee, Maggie!
Hae, there's a ripp to thy auld   *handful –*
   baggie: *stomach*
Tho' thou's howe-backit now' an'   *hollow-backed –*
   knaggie'   *bony*
I've seen the day
Thou could hae gaen like ony staggie,   *colt*
Out-owre the lay.   *lea*

Tho' now thou's dowie, stiff an' crazy'   *drooping*
An' thy auld hide as white's a daisie,
I've seen thee dappl't, sleek an' glaizie,
A bonie gray:
He should been tight that daur't to raize   *excite*
thee,
Ance in a day.

Thou ance was i' the foremost rank,
A filly buirdly, steeve an'   *strong – firm –*
swank;   *stately*
An' set weel down a shapely shank,
As e'er tread yird;   *earth*
An' could hae flown out-owre a stank,   *ditch*
Like ony bird.

It's now some nine-an'-twenty year,
Sin' thou was my guidfather's meere;   *mare*
He gied me thee, o' tocher clear,   *gave – dowry*
An' fifty mark;
Tho' it was sma', 'twas weel-won gear,   *well-earned money*
An' thou was stark.

When first I gaed to woo my Jenny,
Ye then was trottin wi' your minnie: *mother*
Tho' ye was trickie, slee, an' funnie,   *sly*
Ye ne'er was donsie,   *mischievous*
But hamely, tawie, quiet, an' cannie,
An' unco sonsie.   *very plump*

That day, ye pranc'd wi' muckle pride,   *great*
When ye bure hame my bonie bride: *bore*
An' sweet an' gracefu' she did ride,
Wi' maiden air!
Kyle-Stewart I could bragget   *could have bragged*
wide,
For sic a pair.

Tho' now ye dow but hoyte and hobble,   *can — limp*
An' wintle like a saumont-coble,   *twist and rock — salmon-boat*
That day, ye was a jinker noble,   *runner*
For heels an' win'!   *wind*
An' ran them till they a' did wauble,   *reel*
Far, far behin'!

When thou an' I were young an' skiegh,   *high-mettled*
An' stable-meals at fairs were driegh,   *tedious*
How thou wad prance, an' snore, an' skriegh, *whinny*
An' tak the road!
Town's bodies ran, an stood abiegh,   *out of the way*
An' ca't thee mad.   *called*

When thou was corn't, an' I was mellow   *half-tipsy*
We took the road ay like a swallow:
At brooses thou had ne'er a fellow,
For pith an' speed;
But ev'ry tail thou pay't them hollow,
Whare'er thou gaed.

The sma', droop-rumpl't, hunter   *drooping at the crupper*
   cattle
Might aiblins waur't thee   *perhaps beat —*
   for a brattle;   *short race*
But sax Scotch mile, thou try't their mettle,   *six*
An' gar't them whaizle: *made — wheeze*
Nae whip nor spur, but just a wattle   *switch*
O' saugh or hazle.   *willow*

Thou was a noble 'fittie-lan',
As e'er in tug or tow was drawn!
Aft thee an' I, in aught hours' gaun,   *eight hours' work*
On guid March-weather,
Hae turn'd sax rood beside our han',   *six roods*
For days thegither.

Thou never braing't, an' fetch't,   *fretted – raged –*
an' flisket;   *kicked*
But thy auld tail thou wad hae whisket,   *lashed*
An' spread abreed thy weel-fill'd brisket,   *breast*
Wi' pith an' power;
Till sprittie knowes wad rair't an' risket,
An' slypet owre.

When frosts lay lang, an' snaws were deep,   *long*
An' threaten'd labour back to keep,
I gied thy cog a wee bit heap
Aboon the timmer:
I ken'd my Maggie wad na sleep
For that, or simmer.   *before summer*

In cart or car thou never reestet;   *stood still*
The steyest brae thou wad hae fac't it;   *steepest hill*
Thou never lap, an' stenned, an'   *leaped – reared*
breastet,
Then stood to blaw;
But just thy step a wee thing   *a little –*
hastet,   *quickened*
Thou snoov't awa.   *pushed on quietly*

My 'pleugh' is now thy bairn-time a',
Four gallant brutes as e'er did draw;
Forbye sax mae I've sell't awa,   *Besides six more*
That thou has nurst:
They drew me thretteen pund an' twa   *thirteen*
The vera warst.

Mony a sair daurg we twa hae wrought,   *day's work*
An' wi' the weary warl' fought!   *world*
An' mony an anxious day, I thought
We wad be beat!
Yet here to crazy age we're brought,
Wi' something yet.

An' think na', my auld trusty servan',
That now perhaps thou's less deservin,
An' thy auld days may end in starvin,
For my last fow,   *bushel*
A heapet stimpart, I'll reserve ane
Laid by for you.

We've worn to crazy years thegither;
We'll toyte about wi' ane anither;   *move*
Wi' tentie care I'll flit thy tether   *heedful*
To some hain'd rig,   *reserved piece of ground*
Whare ye may nobly rax your leather,   *stretch*
Wi' sma fatigue.

Willie brew'd a Peck o' Maut

While staying at Moffat in Dumfriesshire in September 1787,
Burns's friend William Nicol had his peace disturbed by Burns
and Allan Masterton. With the help of generous quantities of old
John Barleycorn they turned his quiet evening into a night of
mindless merriment. Determined to commemorate the occasion,
Burns and Masterton set to work immediately to produce this
song, with Burns writing the lyrics and Masterton providing the
tune.

Willie brew'd a Peck o' Maut

O Willie brew'd a peck o' maut,	*malt*
And Rob and Allan cam to pree;	*taste*
Three blyther hearts, that lee-lang night,	*livelong*
Ye wad na found in Christendie.	

Chorus – We are na fou, we're nae that fou,	*full*
But just a drappie on our e'e;	*drop – eye*
The cock may craw, the day may daw,	*dawn*
And ay we'll taste the barley bree.	*brew, juice*

Here are we met, three merry boys,
Three merry boys, I trow, are we;
And mony a night we've merry been,
And mony mae we hope to be!   *more*

It is the moon, I ken her horn,	
That's blinkin' in the lift sae hie;	*heavens – high*
She shines sae bright to wyle us hame,	*lure*
But, by my sooth, she'll wait a wee!	*a while*

Wha first shall rise to gang awa,	
A cuckold, coward loun is he!	*fellow*
Wha last beside his chair shall fa',	
He is the King amang us three!	

Address to the Unco Guid,
or the Rigidly Righteous

Written in 1786, probably after Burns had been disciplined for fornication by the Kirk Session of Mauchline Parish Church, the poem is not so much a plea for human frailty as the poet cocking-a-snook at the self-righteous burghers of Mauchline. Debunking the sanctimonious was one of Burns's favourite themes and if we look back to 1784 and into his First Commonplace Book, where he jotted down his thoughts and ideas about life, we can see the seeds of this later work:

Let any of the strictest character for regularity of conduct among us, examine impartially how many of his virtues are owing to constitution and education; how many vices he has never been guilty of, not from any care or vigilance, but from want of opportunity, or some accidental circumstance intervening; how many of the weaknesses of mankind he has escaped because he was out of line of such temptation; and, what often, if not always, weighs more than all the rest; how much he is indebted to the world's good opinion because the world does not know all: I say any man who can thus think, will scan the failings, nay the faults and crimes, of mankind around him, with a brother's eye.

Address to the Unco Guid, or the Rigidly Righteous

My son, these Maxims make a rule,
And lump them ay thegither;   *together*
The *Rigid Righteous* is a fool,
The *Rigid Wise* anither:
The cleanest corn that e'er was
   dight   *thrashed or winnowed*
May hae some pyles o' caff in   *grains – chaff*
So ne'er a fellow-creature slight
For random fits o' daffin.   *merriment, folly*

          Solomon – Eccles. vii. 16.

O ye wha are sae guid yoursel,
Sae pious and sae holy,
Ye've nought to do but mark and tell
Your Neebour's fauts and folly!   *faults*
Whase life is like a weel-gaun mill,   *well-going*
Supply'd wi' store o' water,
The heapèt happer's ebbing still,   *hopper*
And still the clap plays clatter.

Hear me, ye venerable Core,   *folk*
As counsel for poor mortals,
That frequent pass douce Wisdom's door   *grave*
For glaikit Folly's portals;   *careless*
I, for their thoughtless, careless sakes,
Would here propone defences,
Their donsie tricks, their black
    mistakes,   *unlucky*
Their failings and mischances.

Ye see your state wi' theirs compar'd,
And shudder at the niffer,   *comparison*
But cast a moment's fair regard,
What maks the mighty differ;   *difference*
Discount what scant occasion gave,
That purity ye pride in,
And (what's aft mair than a'   *often more –*
    the lave)   *rest*
Your better art o' hiding.

Think, when your castigated pulse
Gies now and then a wallop,   *plunge, flourish*
What ragings must his veins convulse,
That still eternal gallop:
Wi' wind and tide fair i' your tail,
Right on ye scud your sea-way;
But in the teeth o' baith to sail,   *both*
It maks an unco leeway.   *terrible*

See Social-life and Glee sit down,
All joyous and unthinking,
Till, quite transmugrify'd, they're
    grown   *transformed*
Debauchery and Drinking:
O would they stay to calculate
Th' eternal consequences;
Or your more dreaded h–ll to state,
D–mnation of expences!

Ye high, exalted, virtuous Dames,
Ty'd up in godly laces,
Before ye gie poor *Frailty* names,
Suppose a change o' cases;
A dear-lov'd lad, convenience snug,
A treacherous inclination –
But, let me whisper i' your lug,   *ear*
Ye're aiblins nae temptation.   *perhaps*

Then gently scan your brother Man,
Still gentler sister Woman;
Tho' they may gang a kennin wrang,
To step aside is human:
One point must still be greatly dark,
The moving *Why* they do it;
And just as lamely can ye mark,
How far perhaps they rue it.

Who made the heart,' tis *He* alone
Decidedly can try us,
He knows each chord its various tone,
Each spring its various bias:
Then at the balance let's be mute,
We never can adjust it;
What's *done* we partly may compute
But know not what's *resisted*.

A Red, Red Rose

Written in 1794 this song is one of the all-time favourites for the Burns Supper. By combining a lover's parting song he found in an old anthology with a farewell written by a Lieutenant Hinches to his sweetheart, Burns has produced a lasting testament to the pain of parting.

A Red, Red Rose
Tune – Graham's Strathspey

O my Luve's like a red, red rose
That's newly sprung in June;
O my Luve's like the melodie
That's sweetly play'd in tune.
As fair art thou, my bonie lass,
So deep in luve am I;
And I will luve thee still, my dear,
Till a' the seas gang dry.

Till a' the seas gang dry, my Dear,
And the rocks melt wi' the sun;
O I will love thee still, my dear,
While the sands o' life shall run.
And fare thee weel, my only Luve!
And fare thee weel a while!
And I will come again, my Luve,
Tho' it were ten thousand mile!

To a Mouse

One of his best works and a must for most suppers, this poem shows Burns's sympathies extending beyond mankind to all his fellow creatures trying to overcome the frailty of existence. With simplicity and tenderness he demonstrates his empathy for the mouse and its new-found homelessness and reflects on similar feelings and experiences of his own. The well-known proverb from the poem, 'The best-laid schemes o' Mice an' Men gang aft a-gley' sums up his conclusions about life.

The incident which inspired the poem happened in November 1785, when Burns ploughed up a mouse's nest and only just managed to stop John Blane, the boy driving the horses, from killing his 'fellow-mortal'.

To a Mouse

On turning her up in her nest, with the plough, November 1785

Wee, sleekit, cowrin, tim'rous beastie,   *sleek*
O, what a panic's in thy breastie!
Thou need na start awa sae hasty,
Wi' bickering brattle!   *hasty scamper*
I wad be laith to rin an' chase thee,   *loath*
Wi' murd'ring pattle!

I'm truly sorry Man's dominion
Has broken Nature's social union,
An' justifies that ill opinion,
Which makes thee startle,
At me, thy poor, earth-born companion,
An' fellow-mortal!

I doubt na, whyles, but thou may thieve;   *sometimes*
What then? poor beastie, thou maun live!
A daimen icker in a thrave
'S a sma' request:
I'll get a blessin wi' the lave,   *remainder*
And never miss't!

Thy wee bit housie, too, in ruin!
Its silly wa's the win's are strewin!
An' naething, now, to big a new ane,   *erect*
O' foggage green!   *moss*
An' bleak December's winds ensuin,
Baith snell and keen!   *biting*

Thou saw the fields laid bare an' waste,
An' weary Winter comin fast,
An' cozie here, beneath the blast,   *comfortable*
Thou thought to dwell,
Till crash! the cruel coulter past
Out thro' thy cell.

That wee bit heap o' leaves an' stibble,   *stubble*
Has cost thee mony a weary nibble!
Now thou's turn'd out, for a' thy trouble,
But house or hald,   *Without – holding*
To thole the Winter's sleety dribble,   *endure – dribble*
An' cranreuch cauld!   *hoar-frost*

But Mousie, thou art no thy lane,   *not alone*
In proving foresight may be vain:
The best-laid schemes o' Mice an' Men
Gang aft a-gley,   *go often wrong*
An' lea'e us nought but grief and pain,   *leave*
For promis'd joy.

Still thou art blest, compar'd wi' me!
The present only toucheth thee:
But, Och! I backward cast my e'e,
On prospects drear!
An' forward, tho' I canna see,
I guess an' fear!

The Rigs o' Barley

This well-known song comes from Burns's early years at Lochlie Farm. His neighbour, John Rankine, at Adamhill Farm, had a daughter called Annie, who always maintained she was the heroine of the song, but most of the Annies in the district said the same.

Burns believed the last verse to be the best he had ever written, coming nearest to his idea of 'poetical perfection'. A celebration of the rural pleasures of midsummer, it seems essentially Burns.

The Rigs o' Barley
Tune – Corn Riggs

Chorus – Corn Riggs, an' barley riggs,
An' corn riggs are bonie:
I'll ne'er forget that happy night,
Amang the riggs wi' Annie.

It was upon a Lammas night,
When corn riggs are bonie,
Beneath the moon's unclouded light,
I held awa to Annie;
The time flew by, wi' tentless heed,
Till 'tween the late and early,
Wi' sma' persuasion she agreed
To see me thro' the barley.

The sky was blue, the wind was still,
The moon was shining clearly;
I set her down, wi' right good will,
Amang the riggs o' barley:
I ken't her heart was a' my ain;
I lov'd her most sincerely;
I kiss'd her owre and owre again,
Amang the riggs o' barley.

I lock'd her in my fond embrace;
Her heart was beating rarely:
My blessings on that happy place,
Amang the riggs o' barley!
But by the moon and stars so bright,
That shone that hour so clearly!
She ay shall bless that happy night
Amang the riggs o' barley.

I hae been blythe wi' comrades dear;
I hae been merry drinking;
I hae been joyfu' gath'rin gear;
I hae been happy thinking:
But a' the pleasures e'er I saw,
Tho' three times doubl'd fairly –
That happy night was worth them a'
Amang the riggs o' barley.

The Cotter's Saturday Night

Very few Burns Suppers are complete without this poem.
Burns's idyllic scene of the labouring family gathered in the
cottage on a Saturday night has been reproduced on canvas by
many different artists. It certainly has a pictorial quality, and no
doubt Burns was aiming to record for posterity the solid, simple
values of the Scottish rural family. It is Burns's tribute to his
father (William Burnes is the father in the poem) and to the way
of life lived by Burns and many of his fellow Scots. It is at once
personal, parochial and nationalistic, its sentiments reflecting a

people and their staunch beliefs: a God-fearing life, the bonds of kinship and loyalty to one's country.

It was written at Mossgiel in 1785 during his great creative period, almost a year after his father's death.

The Cotter's Saturday Night
Inscribed to R. Aiken, Esq

Let not Ambition mock their useful toil,
Their homely joys, and destiny obscure;
Nor Grandeur hear, with a disdainful smile,
The short and simple annals of the poor.
                                        Gray

My lov'd, my honor'd, much respected friend!
No mercenary bard his homage pays;
With honest pride, I scorn each selfish end,
My dearest meed, a friend's esteem and praise:
To you I sing, in simple Scottish lays,
The lowly train in life's sequester'd scene;
The native feelings strong, the guileless ways;
What Aiken in a cottage would have been;
Ah! tho' his worth unknown, far happier there I ween!

November chill blaws loud wi' angry sugh;   *whistling sound*
The short'ning winter-day is near a close;
The miry beasts retreating frae the pleugh;
The black'ning trains o' craws to their repose: *crows*
The toil-worn Cotter frae his labor goes, –
This night his weekly moil is at an end,
Collects his spades, his mattocks, and his hoes,
Hoping the morn in ease and rest to spend,
And weary, o'er the moor, his course does
    hameward bend.

At length his lonely cot appears in view,
Beneath the shelter of an aged tree;
Th' expectant wee-things, toddlin, stacher through   *stagger*
To meet their 'dad', wi' flitcherin' noise and glee.   *fluttering*
His wee bit ingle blinking bonilie,
His clean hearth-stane, his thrifty wifie's smile,
The lisping infant, prattling on his knee,
Does a' his weary kiaugh and care beguile,   *anxiety*
And make him quite forget his labor and his toil.

Belyve, the elder bairns come drappin in,   *By-and-by*
At service out, amang the farmers roun';
Some ca' the pleugh, some herd, some
    tentie rin   *attentively*
A cannie errand to a neibor town;   *private*
Their eldest hope, their Jenny, woman-grown,
In youthfu' bloom – love sparkling in her e'e –
Comes hame; perhaps, to shew a braw new gown,
Or deposite her sair-won penny-fee,   *hard-earned wages*
To help her parents dear, if they in hardship be.

With joy unfeign'd, brothers and sisters meet,
And each for other's welfare kindly spiers: *inquires*
The social hours, swift-wing'd, unnotic'd fleet;
Each tells the uncos that he sees or hears.   *news*
The parents partial eye their hopeful years;
Anticipation forwards points the view;
The mother, wi' her needle and her sheers,
Gars auld claes look amaist as weel's   *Makes – clothes*
    the new;
The father mixes a' wi' admonition due.

Their master's and their mistress's command,
The younkers a' are warnèd to obey;
And mind their labors wi' an eydent hand,   *diligent*
And ne'er tho' out o' sight, to jauk or play;   *dally*
'And O! be sure to fear the Lord Alway,
Lest in temptation's path ye gang astray,
Implore His counsel and assisting might:
They never sought in vain that sought the Lord aright!'

But hark! a rap comes gently to the door;
Jenny, wha kens the meaning o' the same,
Tells how a neibor lad came o'er the moor,
To do some errands, and convoy her hame.
The wily mother sees the conscious flame
Sparkle in Jenny's e'e, and flush her cheek;
With heart-struck anxious care, enquires his name,
While Jenny hafflins is afraid to speak;   *almost*
Weel-pleas'd the mother hears, it's nae wild,
   worthless rake.

Wi' kindly welcome, Jenny brings him ben;
A strappin' youth, he takes the mother's eye;
Blythe Jenny sees the visit's no ill ta'en;   *received*
The father cracks of horses, pleughs, and kye.
The younster's artless heart o'erflows wi' joy,
But blate an' laithfu', scarce can   *bashful – hesitating*
   weel behave;
The mother, wi' a woman's wiles, can spy
What makes the youth sae bashfu' and sae grave;
Weel-pleas'd to think her bairn's respected like   *child –*
   the lave.   *rest*

O happy love! where love like this is found:
O heart-felt raptures! bliss beyond compare!
I've pacèd much this weary, mortal round,
And sage experience bids me this declare, –
'If Heaven a draught of heavenly pleasure spare –
One cordial in this melancholy vale,
'Tis when a youthful, loving, modest pair
In other's arms, breathe out the tender tale,
Beneath the milk-white thorn that scents the
   evening gale.'

Is there, in human form, that bears a heart,
A wretch! a villain! lost to love and truth!
That can, with studied, sly, ensnaring art,
Betray sweet Jenny's unsuspecting youth?
Curse on his perjur'd arts! dissembling, smooth!
Are honor, virtue, conscience, all exil'd?
Is there no pity, no relenting ruth,
Points to the parents fondling o'er their child?
Then paints the ruin'd maid, and their
    distraction wild?

But now the supper crowns their simple board,
The halesome parritch, chief of Scotia's food;   *porridge*
The sowpe their only hawkie does afford,   *food – cow*
That, 'yont the hallan snugly chows her cood: *porch – cud*
The dame brings forth, in complimental mood,
To grace the lad, her
    weel-hain'd kebbuck, fell;   *well-matured cheese, tasty*
And aft he's prest, and aft he ca's it guid;
The frugal wifie, garrulous, will tell
How 'twas a towmond auld, sin'   *twelvemonth –*
    lint was i' the bell.   *flax in flower*

The cheerfu' supper done, wi' serious face,
They, round the ingle, form a circle wide;
The sire turns o'er, with patriarchal grace,
The big ha'-bible, ance his   *large Bible, that*
    father's pride: *lay in the hall*
His bonnet rev'rently is laid aside,
His lyart haffets wearing thin and bare;   *grey side-locks*
Those strains that once did sweet in Zion glide,
He wales a portion with judicious care;   *selects*
And 'Let us worship God!' he says with solemn air.

They chant their artless notes in simple guise,
They tune their hearts, by far the noblest aim;
Perhaps 'Dundee's' wild-warbling measures rise,
Or plaintive 'Martyrs,' worthy of the name;

Or noble 'Elgin' beets the heaven-ward flame,   *fans*
The sweetest far of Scotia's holy lays:
Compar'd with these, Italian trills are tame;
The tickl'd ears no heart-felt raptures raise;
Nae unison hae they, with our Creator's praise.

The priest-like father reads the sacred page,
How Abram was the friend of God on high;
Or, Moses bade eternal warfare wage
With Amalek's ungracious progeny;
Or, how the royal bard did groaning lie
Beneath the stroke of Heaven's avenging ire;
Or Job's pathetic plaint, and wailing cry;
Or rapt Isaiah's wild, seraphic fire;
Or other holy seers that tune the sacred lyre.

Perhaps the Christian volume is the theme,
How guiltless blood for guilty man was shed;
How He, who bore in Heaven the second name,
Had not on earth whereon to lay His head:
How His first followers and servants sped;
The precepts sage they wrote to many a land:
How he, who lone in Patmos banishèd,
Saw in the sun a mighty angel stand,
And heard great Bab'lon's doom pronounc'd by
    Heaven's command.

Then kneeling down to Heaven's Eternal King,
The saint, the father, and the husband prays:
Hope 'springs exulting on triumphant wing,'
That thus they all shall meet in future days,
There, ever bask in uncreated rays,
No more to sigh, or shed the bitter tear,
Together hymning their Creator's praise,
In such society, yet still more dear;
While circling Time moves round in an eternal sphere.

Compar'd with this, how poor Religion's pride,
In all the pomp of method, and of art;
When men display to congregations wide
Devotion's ev'ry grace, except the heart!
The Power, incens'd, the pageant will desert,
The pompous strain, the sacredotal stole;
But haply, in some cottage far apart,
may hear, well pleas'd, the language of the soul;
And in His Book of Life the inmates poor enroll.

Then homeward all take off their sev'ral way;
The youngling cottagers retire to rest: *youthful*
The parent-pair their secret homage pay,
And proffer up to Heaven the warm request,
That He who stills the raven's cam'rous nest,
And decks the lily fair in flow'ry pride,
Would, in the way His wisdom sees the best,
For them and for their little ones provide;
But chiefly, in their hearts with grace divine preside.

From scenes like these, old Scotia's grandeur springs,
That makes her lov'd at home, rever'd abroad:
Princes and lords are but the breath of kings,
'An honest man's the noblest work of God;'
And certes, in fair virtue's heavenly road,
The cottage leaves the place far behind;
What is a lordling's pomp? – a cumbrous load,
Disguising oft the wretch of human kind,
Studied in arts of hell, in wickedness refin'd!

O Scotia! my dear, my native soil!
For whom my warmest wish to Heaven is sent,
Long may thy hardy sons of rustic toil
Be blest with health, and peace, and sweet content!
And O! may Heaven their simple lives prevent
From luxury's contagion, weak and vile!
Then, howe'er crowns and coronets be rent,
A virtuous populace may rise the while,
And stand a wall of fire around their much-lov'd
   isle.

O Thou! who pour'd the patriotic tide,
That stream'd thro' Wallace's undaunted heart,
Who dar'd to, nobly, stem tyrannic pride,
Or nobly die, the second glorious part:
(The patriot's God, peculiarly thou art,
His friend, inspirer, guardian, and reward!)
O never, never, Scotia's realm desert;
But still the patriot, and the patriot-bard,
In bright succession raise, her ornament and guard!

Bruce to his Men at Bannockburn

In 1314 King Edward II's 18 000-strong army was resoundingly
defeated by Robert the Bruce's 8000 men at the Battle of
Bannockburn. Burns composed this imaginary address by Bruce
to his soldiers on the morning of the battle, setting it to the air
'Hey tuttie, taitie', believed to be Bruce's marching tune. Burns
said it often moved him to tears. He visited the site of the battle
in 1787 and visualized his 'gallant, heroic countrymen, coming
o'er the hill and down upon the plunderers of their country'.

Burns composed the song in September 1793 and sent it to
George Thomson for his *Select Scottish Airs*. Thomson persuaded
him to change the tune to 'Lewie Gordon', but public demand
ensured that Burns's original choice was reinstated.

Bruce to his Men at Bannockburn
Tune – Hey, tuttie, taitie

Scots, wha hae wi' Wallace bled,   *who have*
Scots, wham Bruce has aften led,   *whom*
Welcome to your gory bed
Or to victorie!

Now's the day, and now's the hour;
See the front of battle lour;
See approach proud Edward's power –
Chains and slaverie!

Wha will be a traitor-knave?
Wha can fill a coward's grave?
Wha sae base as be a slave?
Let him turn and flee!

Wha for Scotland's king and law
Freedom's sword will strongly draw,
Freeman stand, or freeman fa',
Let him follow me!

By oppression's woes and pains!
By your sons in servile chains!
We will drain our dearest veins,
But they shall be free!

Lay the proud usurpers low!
Tyrants fall in ev'ry foe!
Liberty's in ev'ry blow! –
Let us do or die!

The Evening Ends

Brief speeches of thanks

As the evening draws to a close the Chairman has a few final duties to perform. First, he calls on a club member or official to thank all the participants in the festivities. This should include thanking the Chairman himself, the Secretary and all those who took part in the preparations.

'Auld Lang Syne'

Finally, the Chairman asks the company to stand, link hands and to join in the singing of 'Auld Lang Syne'. Burns added the third and fourth verses to this ancient air, making it universally his own. He composed his version of the song in 1788. Now an international anthem, it is sung at the close of gatherings all over the world. Its charm lies in the easy intimacy and simplicity of the lyrics, the remembrance of old friendships and the desire to be transported back to the days of childhood.

Auld Lang Syne

Should auld acquaintance be forgot,   *old*
And never brought to mind?
Should auld acquaintance be forgot,
And auld lang syne!   *days of long ago*

Chorus – For auld lang syne, my dear,
            For auld lang syne,
            We'll tak a cup o' kindness yet,
            For auld lang syne.

And surely ye'll be your pint stowp!   *tankard*
And surely I'll be mine!
And we'll tak a cup o' kindness yet,
For auld lang syne.

We twa hae run about the braes,
And pou'd the gowans fine: *pulled*
But we've wander'd mony a weary fitt,   *many – foot*
Sin' auld lang syne.   *Since*

We twa hae paidl'd in the burn   *waded*
Frae morning sun till dine: *dinner-time*
But seas between us braid hae roar'd   *broad*
Sin' auld lang syne.

And there's a hand, my trusty fiere!   *friend*
And gie's a hand o' thine!   *give*
And we'll tak a right gude willie-waught   *draught*
For auld lang syne.

Mill Vennel, Dumfries (now Burns Street)

Final Details

At this point, unless a dance is planned for the remainder of the evening, the supper draws to a close and the guests depart having thoroughly enjoyed a unique and uplifting occasion. It remains only for the organizers to send letters of thanks to those participants whose efforts have contributed to the evening's success and inform the local press that the supper has been a lively and enjoyable high point in the community's annual list of events. Community involvement, of course, is very much at the heart of the Burns movement, with the Burns Federation promoting the poet's memory and work through schools, lectures and competitions and the Jean Armour Burns Houses and National Burns Memorial Homes, in the district of Mauchline, providing shelter for those in need of a place to spend their final years. Through endeavours of this kind Burns's thoughts and love of his fellow man are turned into deeds by those who share his concern for the less fortunate. This is his true memorial. For further information contact:

The Burns Federation,
   Dick Institute, Elmbank Avenue, Kilmarnock KA1 3BU

Quotations

The following selection of prose and poetry should prove useful to the speechmaker. The quotations have been organized under the headings of mankind, religion, fortune, the lasses, love, drink, wisdom and Burns's beliefs. Many others could be selected.

Burns himself was an enthusiastic collector of quotations as his poems and letters demonstrate and the following extract testifies:

I like to have quotations ready for every occasion. – They give one's ideas so pat, and save one the trouble of finding expression adequate to one's feelings.
(Letter to Agnes McLehose, Edinburgh, 14 January 1788)

Mankind

Lord! What is man? What a bustling little bundle of passions, appetites, ideas and fancies!
(From Gordon Irving, *The Wit of Robert Burns*)

> Ye'll try the world soon, my lad,
> And Andrew dear, believe me,
> Ye'll find mankind an unco squad,   *strange crew*
> And muckle they may grieve ye: *much*
> (*Epistle to a Young Friend*)

> Conceal yoursel as weel's ye can   *well*
> Frae critical dissection;   *from*
> But keek thro' ev'ry other man   *look searchingly*
> Wi' sharpen'd, sly inspection.
> (*Epistle to a Young Friend*)

O ye wha are sae guid yoursel,
Sae pious and sae holy,
Ye've nought to do but mark and tell
Your Neebour's fauts and folly!   *faults*
(*Address to the Unco Guid*)

'O Man! while in thy early years,
How prodigal of time!
Mis-spending all thy precious hours,
Thy glorious youthful prime!
(*Man was made to mourn*)

They gie the wit of age to youth;
They let us ken oursel;
They make us see the naked truth –
The real guid and ill:
Tho' losses an' crosses
Be lessons right severe,
There's wit there, ye'll get there,
Ye'll find nae other where.
(*Epistle to Davie*)

Religion

When ranting round in Pleasure's ring   *making merry*
Religion may be blinded;
Or if she gie a random sting,   *give*
It may be little minded;
But when on Life we're tempest-driv'n,
A Conscience but a canker –
A correspondence fix'd wi' Heav'n,
Is sure a noble anchor!
(*Epistle to a Young Friend*)

By the bye, I intend breeding him [Burns's eldest son] up
for the Church; and from an innate dexterity in secret
Mischief which he possesses and a certain hypocritical
gravity as he looks on the consequence, I have no small
hopes of him in the sacerdotal line.
(Letter to Alexander Cunningham, Ellisland, 27 July 1788)

One thing frightens me much: that we are to live for ever, seems too good news to be true. – That we are to enter into a new scene of existence, where exempt from want and pain we shall enjoy ourselves and our friends without satiety or separation – how much would I be indebted to any one who could fully assure me that this were certain fact!
(Letter to Alexander Cunningham, Ellisland, 14 January 1790)

All my fears and cares are of this world: if there is Another, an honest man has nothing to fear from it.
(Letter to Alexander Cunningham, Ellisland, 14 February 1790)

> L–d hear my earnest cry and pray'r
> Against that Presbytry of Ayr!
> Thy strong right hand, L–d make it bare
> Upo' their heads!
> L–d visit them and dinna spare,
> For their misdeeds!
> (*Holy Willie's Prayer*)

Fortune

> To catch Dame Fortune's golden smile,
> Assiduous wait upon her;
> And gather gear by ev'ry wile   *wealth*
> That's justify'd by Honor:
> (*Epistle to a Young Friend*)

Then sore harass'd, and tir'd at last, with Fortune's vain delusion,
I dropt my schemes, like idle dreams, and came to this
   conclusion –
The past was bad, and the future hid – its good or ill untried;
But the present hour was in my pow'r, and so I would enjoy it.
(*My Father was a Farmer*)

Fortune has so much forsaken me that she has taught me to live without her.
(Letter to Charles Sharpe, Dumfries, 22 April 1791)

> The honest heart that' free frae a'
> Intended fraud or guile,
> However Fortune kick the ba',   ball
> Has ay some cause to smile;
> (*Epistle to Davie*)

All you who follow wealth and power with unremitting ardour,
The more in this you look for bliss, you leave your view the farther:
Had you the wealth Potosi boasts, or nations to adore you,
A cheerful honest-hearted clown I will prefer before you.
(*My Father was a Farmer*)

The Lasses

> But gie me a cannie hour at e'en,   happy
> My arms about my dearie, O;
> An' war'ly cares, an' war'ly men,
> May a' gae tapsalteerie, O!   topsy-turvy
> (*Green grow the Rashes*)

> Auld Nature swears, the lovely dears
> Her noblest work she classes, O:
> Her prentice han' she try'd on man,
> An' then she made the lasses, O.
> (*Green grow the Rashes*)

The charms o' the min', the langer they shine,   mind
The mair admiration they draw, man;
While peaches and cherries, and roses and lilies,
They fade and they wither awa, man.
(*The Ronalds of the Bennals*)

Tho' women's minds, like winter winds,
May shift, and turn, an' a' that,
The noblest breast adores them maist,   *most*
A consequence I draw that.
(song: *For a' That an' a' That*)

When ance life's day draws near the   *once —*
    gloamin,   *twilight*
Then fareweel vacant, careless roamin;
An' fareweel cheerfu' tankards foamin,
An' social noise:
An' fareweel dear, deluding woman,
The joy of joys!
(*Epistle to James Smith*)

Awa' wi' your witchcraft o' beauty's alarms,
The slender bit beauty you grasp in your arms;
O gie me the lass that has acres o' charms,
O gie me the lass wi' the
    weel-stockit farms.   *well-stocked*
(*Hey for a Lass wi' a Tocher*)

Lassie wi' the lint-white locks,
Bonie lassie, artless lassie,
Wilt thou wi' me tent the flocks   *herd*
Wilt thou be my Dearie O?
(*Lassie wi' the Lint-white Locks*)

Love

Till a' the seas gang dry, my Dear,
And the rocks melt wi' the sun;
O I will love thee still, my dear,
While the sands o' life shall run.
And fare thee weel, my only Luve!
And fare thee weel a while!
And I will come again, my Luve,
Tho' it were ten thousand mile!
(*A Red, Red Rose*)

Flow gently, sweet Afton, among thy green
    braes,   *hill-slope*
Flow gently, I'll sing thee a song in thy praise;
My Mary's asleep by thy murmuring stream,
Flow gently, sweet Afton, disturb not her dream.
(*Afton Water*)

Hers are the willing chains o' love,
By conquering Beauty's sovereign law:
And still my Chloris' dearest charm —
She says she lo'es me best of a'.
(*She says she lo'es me Best of A'*)

Then come, thou fairest of the fair,
Those wonted smiles O let me share;
And by thy beauteous self I swear
No love but thine my heart shall know.
(*Fairest Maid on Devon Banks*)

Had we never loved sae kindly!
Had we never lov'd sae blindly!
Never met — or never parted,
We had ne'er been broken-hearted.
(*Ae Fond Kiss*)

Ae fond kiss, and then we sever!
Ae fareweel, Alas, for ever!
Deep in heart-wrung tears I'll pledge thee,
Warring sighs and groans I'll wage thee.
(*Ae Fond Kiss*)

Misery is like Love; to speak its language truly, the Author
must have felt it.
(From Gordon Irving, *The Wit of Robert Burns*)

Drink

John Barleycorn was a hero bold,
Of noble enterprise;
For if you do but taste his blood,
'Twill make your courage rise.
(*John Barleycorn*)

Inspiring bold John Barleycorn!
What dangers thou canst make us scorn!
Wi' tippenny, we fear nae evil;
Wi' usquabae we'll face the devil!   *whisky*
(Tam o' Shanter)

We are na fou, we're nae that fou,   *drunk*
But just a drappie on our e'e   *drop – eye*
The cock may craw, the day may daw,   *dawn*
And ay we'll taste the barley bree.   *brew, juice*
(*Willie brew'd a Peck o' Maut*)

The clachan yill had made me canty,   *village ale – merry*
I was na fou, but just had plenty;   *drunk*
I stacher'd whyles, but yet took   *staggered at times –*
    tent ay   *care*
To free the ditches;
An' hillocks, stanes, an' bushes, kenn'd ay
Frae ghaists an' witches.
(*Death and Dr Hornbook*)

Leeze me on drink! it gies us
    mair   *Commend me to*
Than either school or college;
It kindles wit, it waukens lear,   *rouses – learning*
It pangs us fou o' knowledge   *crams – full*
Be 't whisky-gill or
    penny-wheep,   *very small beer*
Or ony stronger potion,
It never fails, on drinkin deep,
To kittle up our notion,   *enliven our wits*
By night or day.
(*The Holy Fair*)

See Social-life and Glee sit down,
All joyous and unthinking
Till, quite transmugrify'd, they're
    grown   *transformed*
Debauchery and Drinking.
(*Address to the Unco Guid*)

The Whisky of this country is a most rascally liquor; and by consequence, only drunk by the most rascally part of the inhabitants.
(Letter to John Tennant Jr, Ellisland, 22 December 1788)

Freedom and whisky gan thegither!   *go together*
Tak aff your dram!
(*The Author's Earnest Cry and Prayer*)

Wisdom

Gie me ae spark o' nature's fire,
That's a' the learning I desire;
Then tho' I drudge thro' dub an' mire   *puddles*
At pleugh or cart,
My muse, tho' hamely in attire,
May touch the heart.
(*Epistle to J. Lapraik*)

But pleasures are like poppies spread,
You seize the flow'r, its bloom is shed;
Or like the snow falls in the river,
A moment white – then melts for ever;
(*Tam o' Shanter*)

Life is all a variorum,
We regard not how it goes;
Let them cant about decorum,
Who have character to lose.
(*The Jolly Beggars*)

But human bodies are sic fools,
For a' their colleges an' schools,
That when nae real ills perplex them,
They mak enow themsels to vex them; *enough*
(*The Twa Dogs*)

But Mousie, thou art no thy lane, *not alone*
In proving foresight may be vain:
The best-laid schemes o' Mice an' Men
Gang aft a-gley, *go often wrong*
An' lea'e us nought but grief and pain, *leave*
For promised joy.
(*To a Mouse*)

Life is but a Day at most;
Sprung from Night – in Darkness lost:
Hope not Sunshine every hour,
Fear not Clouds will ever lour.
Happiness is but a name,
Make Content and Ease thy aim.
Ambition is a meteor-gleam;
Fame, a restless, idle dream;
(*Written in Friars' Carse Hermitage*)

If happiness hae not her seat,
An' centre in the breast,
We may be wise, or rich, or great,
But never can be blest;
Nae treasures nor pleasures
Could make us happy lang;
The heart ay's the part ay *always*
That makes us right or wrang.
(*Epistle to Davie*)

Burns's beliefs

A Mathematician without Religion is a probable character;
an irreligious Poet is a Monster.
(Letter to Mrs Dunlop, Edinburgh, 12 February 1788)

Those who think that composing a Scotch song is a trifling business – let them try.
(Letter to James Hoy, 6 November 1787)

Whatever mitigates the woes, or increases the happiness of others, this is my criterion of goodness; and whatever injures society at large, or an individual in it, this is my measure of iniquity.
(Letter to Mrs Dunlop, Edinburgh, 22 June 1789)

In concluding your speech you could use this quote:

I have ever observed that when once people who have nothing to say have fairly set out, they know not when to stop.
(Letter to Robert Maxwell, Ellisland, 20 December 1789).

Bibliography

Chambers, Robert, *The Life and Works of Robert Burns*, Vols I–IV, Chambers, Edinburgh, 1896

Crawford, Thomas, *Burns: A Study of the Poems and Songs*, Oliver and Boyd, Edinburgh, 1960

Daiches, David, *Robert Burns and his World*, Thames and Hudson, London, 1971

DeLancey Ferguson, J. (ed), *The Letters of Robert Burns*, Vols 1–11, Oxford University Press, Oxford, 1931

DeLancey Ferguson, J., *Pride and Passion*, Oxford University Press, Oxford, 1939

Irving, Gordon, (ed), *The Wit of Robert Burns*, Leslie Frewin Publications Ltd, London, 1972

Jack, Ronald D.S. and Andrew Noble (eds), *The Art of Robert Burns*, Vision Press, London, 1982

Keith, Christina, *The Russet Coat*, Robert Hale, London, 1956

Mackay, James A., *The Burns Federation 1885–1995*, the Burns Federation, Kilmarnock, 1985

Snyder, Franklyn Bliss, *The Life of Robert Burns*, Macmillan, London, 1932

Index

Charles Macsween and Son

Macsween of Edinburgh is a Scottish family business which specializes in the production of traditional Scottish haggis – the national dish of Scotland.

For centuries haggis was made in the home, with each family having its own favoured recipe. The Macsween family recipe, handed down from generation to generation, is still used today for those who enjoy 'real' haggis, made mainly by hand and in the natural skin. Great care is taken in the making of this particularly Scottish delicacy and only the finest ingredients are used, including the best locally milled oatmeal.

Thousands of people at home and abroad have tasted, enjoyed and returned for more, and Macsween is proud to be the sole supplier of haggis to many leading UK stores, including Harrods, Fortnum and Mason and, Edinburgh's famous store, Jenners.

Macsween haggis can be purchased over the counter at the Edinburgh shop or by mail order (send a stamped addressed envelope for a price list) and also by phone. Any help with quantities for a Burns Supper or Scottish evening is freely given. The advice is to order as early as possible for a special occasion, to avoid disappointment.

Scotsmen and women everywhere owe a debt of gratitude to Robert Burns for his huge contribution to Scotland's heritage. This debt can best be repaid by keeping alive his vision for mankind with the celebration of his birth every year.

A Burns Supper should be serious and fun at the same time. It can only be this if it is well organized, and Macsween congratulates the author on her efforts to help those who take on this responsible, and sometimes thankless, task. Macsween also thanks all haggis enthusiasts everywhere for their continued support in its efforts to maintain authenticity and quality in the haggis – the centre-piece of this great tradition.

Macsween of Edinburgh
130 Bruntsfield Place, Edinburgh EH10 4ES

Wm Teacher and Sons Ltd

In 1830 William Teacher was employed in a small grocery business in the Anderston area of Glasgow by a lady who was later to become his mother-in-law. He quickly identified his first business opportunity for he persuaded her to take out a liquor licence and set aside a section of the shop for retailing alcoholic drinks.

By 1851 he was listed as a wholesale wine and spirit merchant and had expanded from the original 'take home' retail shops into Dram Shops at which customers could drink on the premises. He and his sons, Adam and William, became extremely skilful in the new business of blending and the quality of their Scotch was a feature of the Dram Shops. They were so successful that other retailers asked them to supply whisky in bulk.

By 1861 there were 18 Teacher Dram Shops in Glasgow and the business was known as William Teacher & Sons.

As the bulk sales of blended whisky developed, increased industrial activity brought more business for everyone.

The company continued to grow rapidly, and in 1884 the *Teacher's Highland Cream* brand name was registered. *Teacher's Highland Cream* was becoming of increasing importance to the business and the exceptional quality of this blend had to be maintained. Adam Teacher decided that the company should establish its own distillery to provide a unique single malt whisky to form the heart of the Highland Cream blend. Accordingly, the building of the Ardmore distillery in Aberdeenshire began in 1897.

The ability of the company to innovate came to the fore once again in 1913. William Manera Bergius, a nephew of Adam Teacher, devised a patent closure that allowed a tapered cork, attached to a wooden head, to be removed by simply twisting and pulling.

This, coupled with a new design bottle and label, was to place *Teacher's Highland Cream Scotch Whisky* before the licensed trade and public in a way that ensured its future. Described in advertising as 'The Self-Opening Bottle', and coupled with advice to 'Bury the Corkscrew', the new packaging provided a lead for everyone in the Scotch whisky industry.

In 1960 Teacher's sold the last of the famous retail shops in Glasgow, for growth had now taken the company in a new direction.

The financing of large reserves of fine whiskies, needed for expansion, requires resources that are only generated by substantial groups. This was provided when, in 1976, Teacher's became part of what is now the Allied-Lyons 'family' of companies and later, in 1987, joined its sister companies in Allied Distillers Limited.

Care and attention to detail, linked with a keen awareness of the society in which the company operated, guided decisions of the founder in the early 19th century. The same principles govern his successors today at St Enoch Square in the heart of Glasgow.